# Backcountry Skiing
# Snoqualmie Pass

## Help Us Keep This Guide Up to Date

Every effort has been made by the author and editors to make this guide as accurate and useful as possible. However, many things can change after a guide is published—trails are rerouted, regulations change, techniques evolve, facilities come under new management, etc.

We would love to hear from you concerning your experiences with this guide and how you feel it could be improved and kept up to date. Although we may not be able to respond to all comments and suggestions, we'll take them to heart and we'll also make certain to share them with the author. Please send your comments and suggestions to the following address:

The Globe Pequot Press
Reader Response/Editorial Department
P.O. Box 480
Guilford, CT 06437

Or you may e-mail us at:

editorial@globe-pequot.com

Thanks for your input, and happy travels!

# Backcountry Skiing
## Snoqualmie Pass

## Martin Volken

FALCON®

Guilford, Connecticut
An imprint of The Globe Pequot Press

Cover photo by Carl Skoog (Mike Hattrup on The Snoqualmie Haute Route)
Text design: Casey Shain
Maps by Tim Kissel

ISSN 1536-3597
ISBN 0-7627-1066-7

 Text pages printed on recycled paper.

Manufactured in the United States of America
First Edition/First Printing

# Contents

## Overnight Tours

## Multiday Tours

## A Bonus Tour

# Acknowledgments

Special thanks to Andy Dappen for making it all readable; to my wife, Gina, for her patience; and to Scott Schell, Peter Avolio, Mike Hattrup, Don Denton, Shane Wilder, Jim Sammet, and Ben Haskell for coming along. I would also like to thank Carl Skoog, Greg Lange, Dave Metallo, Murray Gailbreth, and Chris Solomon.

And very special thanks to Jim Graham for his graphic help and to John Rudder, who generously provided his pilot skills and airplane for the photo flight.

# Legend

| | |
|---|---|
| Interstate Highway | ═══⟨90⟩═══ |
| State or Local Road | ───────── |
| Backcountry Ski Trail | ─ ─ ─ ─ ─ ─ |
| Variation Trail | - - - - - - - - |
| Parking | 🅿 |
| Campground | ⛺ |
| Camp | ▲ |
| Mountain or Peak | △ **Granite Mountain** |
| River or Creek | ‿‿‿‿‿ |
| Waterfall | ‿‿+ǀ·+ǀ+ǀ·‿ǀ‿ |
| Lake | ⬭ |
| Glacier | ⬬ |
| Contour Line and Contour Value | ‿‿ *6000* ‿‿ |

Note:  A contour line is an imaginary line that connects points
of equal elevation. If it were possible to cut level slices
on a mountain with a large knife at uniform intervals,
the edges of the cut would be the contour lines.

The contour value is the distance from sea level.

The contour interval is the vertical distance between
contour lines. Close spacing of contour lines indicates
a steep slope, while contour lines spread out indicate
a gradual slope.

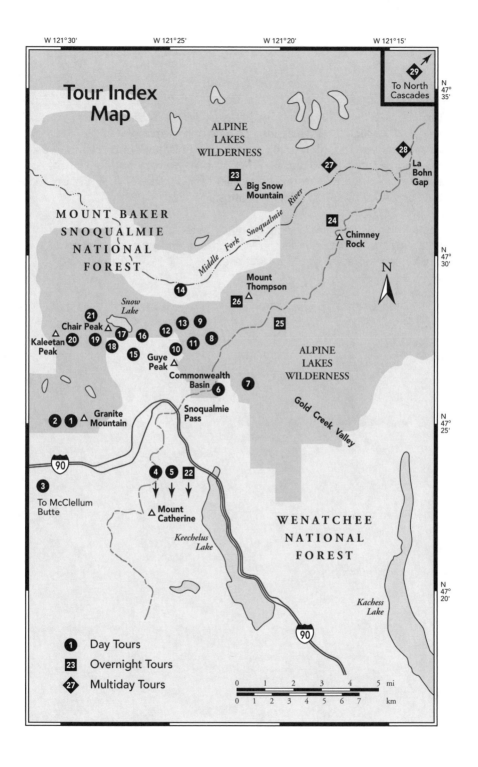

Tour Index
Map

W 121°30'    W 121°25'    W 121°20'    W 121°15'

N 47°35'

To North
Cascades

ALPINE
LAKES
WILDERNESS

MOUNT BAKER
SNOQUALMIE
NATIONAL
FOREST

23
△ Big Snow
Mountain

27

28
La
Bohn
Gap

Middle Fork Snoqualmie River

24
△ Chimney
Rock

N 47°30'

Snow
Lake

Mount
Thompson
26 △

25

N

21
Chair Peak △
Kaleetan
Peak △  20  19  17  16  12  13  9
        18       15  10  11  8

Guye
Peak △

Commonwealth
Basin  6    7

ALPINE
LAKES
WILDERNESS

Gold Creek Valley

Snoqualmie
Pass

2  1  △ Granite
        Mountain

N 47°25'

90

3
To McClellum
Butte

4  5  22

△ Mount
Catherine

Keechelus
Lake

WENATCHEE
NATIONAL
FOREST

N 47°20'

Kachess
Lake

90

●1  Day Tours
■23  Overnight Tours
◆27  Multiday Tours

0   1   2   3   4   5  mi
0  1  2  3  4  5  6  7  km

## CAUTION

Outdoor recreation activities are by their very nature potentially hazardous. All participants in such activities must assume the responsibility for their own actions and safety. The information contained in this guidebook cannot replace sound judgment and good decision-making skills, which help reduce risk exposure, nor does the scope of this book allow for disclosure of all the potential hazards and risks involved in such activities.

Learn as much as possible about the outdoor recreation activities you participate in, prepare for the unexpected, and be safe and cautious. The reward will be a safer and more enjoyable experience.

# Introduction

When I came to the Puget Sound region from Switzerland in 1988, I didn't think much of Snoqualmie Pass. I was raised a few miles from Zermatt and, when I saw the ski areas at the pass, I had something of a snobbish Swiss attitude. The vertical here was moderate, the snow quality was highly questionable, and half the time it seemed to be raining.

After a couple of years, however, I realized that snow was much more common in the Cascades than rain. The cumulative snowfall impressed me, and the challenging little area of Alpental (where style takes a backseat to substance) embodied what skiing was all about. Furthermore, I had never night-skied and found this highly entertaining.

In the early 1990s I began training for the Swiss Mountain Guide exams, and friends would tell me about tours at Stevens Pass, Crystal Mountain, Blewitt Pass, White Pass, or Mount Baker. I discovered, however, that Snoqualmie Pass is hard to beat as an easily accessed midwinter touring destination. The area provides rugged terrain, big relief, forested slopes, gladed bowls, and above-timberline peaks. And while Seattle is very close—less than an hour's drive—I can quickly find complete solitude here.

For all these reasons—and because there is no guide highlighting the more adventurous tours possible at the pass—I decided to prepare this book. I tried to choose tours that held something for ski tourers of varying abilities.

The peaks north of Snoqualmie Pass (with the exception of the Lemah–Chimney Rock massif) may not hold a summer mountaineer's attention for too long, but winter adds the needed alpine element to make these mountains superb ski-mountaineering goals. If you study a topo map, you'll find that this region has a rugged relief rather uncharacteristic of the North Central Cascades. Just a few miles north of the pass are glaciers larger than those of the Stewart Range. This foliated region, extending from Kaleetan Peak to Mount Daniel, offers everything needed to challenge a ski mountaineer.

Over time I've also come to appreciate the area's maritime snowpack. First of all, it's something we can count on. The maritime snow is also responsible for the glaciation in our mountains. Glaciers are created through a sensitive interplay of temperature, precipitation, snow density, and altitude. Most other mountain ranges in the lower 48 lack one of these crucial ingredients and are, therefore, glacier-free (or nearly glacier-free). Having been raised in the Alps, I find mountains without glaciers a bit like pictures without frames.

Even more important, our snowpack is very forgiving. You can consistently ski steeper lines than a continental snowpack allows. And the spring snowpack is often so consolidated that you can cover amazing distances; backcountry travel becomes pure joy.

Don't misunderstand. Even the "high-elasticity snows" of the western Cascades hold many avalanche hazards. That hazard is most ominous in spring, when climax avalanches are most likely. Because we get so much snow, however, slide hazard is often high following a storm or after strong winds have transported fields of snow to new slopes. Furthermore, because our mountains are rained upon, the resulting ice crusts can form hazardous running surfaces for future snows to slide upon. Due to the impressive relief of our mountains, even the same aspect of the same mountain can hold different pockets of snow with different stability characteristics. Finally, the snowpack of the pass isn't always strictly maritime, because colder continental air from the east side sometimes spills across the Cascade crest.

All of this means I will refrain from making generalizations about snow safety in the Cascades: Generalizations lead to disastrous results in the mountains. Several good books about snow science are on the market, and you should read them. But book knowledge isn't enough. To reduce the likelihood of becoming an avalanche statistic, you need experience applying this knowledge in the backcountry, and you need to place heavy emphasis on proper tour planning (more about this later).

People ask me how you can avoid *all* the hidden dangers of the backcountry. You can't. Fortunately, experience and proper tour preparation, combined with an ongoing desire to learn more about the mountain environment, can get you much closer to that goal. This is part of what makes ski touring and ski mountaineering so exciting. They're sports that go far beyond the traditional reasons of why people ski. So much goes into becoming an expert ski mountaineer that you won't get bored with it anytime soon. If you're someone who's drifted slowly out of downhill skiing because you've "done it all," you'll find that ski touring and ski mountaineering take skiing to a new level.

Welcome to this new level—and to a new level of skiing you probably didn't know you'd find at Snoqualmie Pass.

## The Two Religions: Alpine Touring versus Telemarking

People take their skiing styles very seriously. Bumper stickers have even been printed up expressing what amounts almost to two belief systems: Is it FREE YOUR HEEL AND FREE YOUR MIND, or is it FIX YOUR HEEL AND FIX YOUR PROBLEM? There's no absolute answer here because we're talking about attitudes, but I believe that both skiing styles have their place. Furthermore, in many situations, there's no clear-cut "best" system.

I do want to emphasize, however, that too many alpine skiers incorrectly believe that to ski the backcountry you must telemark. I've often talked to expert alpine skiers who wanted to backcountry ski but never did, because they couldn't bear the thought of learning the telemark turn and becoming a beginner all over again. I even had a Boeing engineer come to my ski shop in the winter of 1995, showing me proudly that he was in the process of solving the alpine skier's dilemma. He was inventing a binding that had both a walking and a skiing position. The man was devastated when I told him that he was not

Summit
Chief Col

*Tour 28, The Snoqualmie Haute Route, Day 4*
**Summit Chief Col from south**
*Photo by Martin Volken*

going to strike it rich after all: He was about forty years too late inventing the randonnee (or alpine-touring) binding.

Telemarking was rediscovered in North America in the 1960s and 1970s by skiers who were fed up with the status seeking, glitz, and expense of alpine skiing. These people wanted to return to the genuine article of skiing. They were different from Aspenites and cross-country skiers: Waxes and skins allowed them to tour the backcountry, while the telemark turn allowed them to negotiate (and enjoy) the downhills encountered en route. With this gear, there were no cumbersome boots or bindings; the transition from walking to skiing was effortless. A new generation of free-spirited skiers was born—with folks who professed that they needed less gear, pursued a less contrived sport, and covered a lot more ground than lift-dependent skiers. This was true, but many telemark skiers did not know that in other parts of the world alpine skiers had been backcountry skiing for years on randonnee gear (also called alpine-touring gear).

Let's take a closer look at the history of these two skiing styles. Learning about it helped me shed some of my prejudices, and might do the same for you.

Telemarking originated in Norway in the region of Telemark. The topography of this area is gentler than that of the Alps. Skiers' objectives here were to cover a lot of ground and to negotiate relatively moderate ski descents. Out of utilitarian need evolved a sport whose gear fulfilled both goals fairly well. Skiers could cover ground easily, because the heel was free and the gear was light. Meanwhile, the telemark turn brought skiers down surprisingly steep slopes.

All of Norway agrees that Sondre Norheim was the driving force behind bringing skiing into the modern era. In the mid-1850s he redefined skiing not just as a means of travel or a weapon of war, but as a sport. About this time Norwegians were holding ski competitions, and Norheim was consistently besting the field with the telemark turn—which he either invented or greatly refined. Besides great strides in technique, Norheim made great technological strides as well. He was the innovator who took bindings from a simple leather strap (which had skis being worn like clogs) to a stiffer fixture with a heel strap that, for the first time, allowed lateral pressure to be applied to skis. He's recognized as the inventor of sidecut and of the concept that a "waisted" ski turns itself more willingly.

In Norheim's time the usual form of "slalam"—as the Norwegians called the burgeoning sport of recreational skiing—was to travel across open country, over stone fences, down hillocks, and in and out of thickets of brush. Norheim, however, was known for his love of what was called "the reckless track" (gotta love that term), which involved descents of steep slopes, jumps over rocks, and runs in and out of trees. Let's just call it free skiing. Or extreme skiing.

As if that weren't enough, Norheim tinkered with the dimensions of his skis. In his day skis were often 10 feet long, and he cut a whopping 2 feet off their length. He also gave his boards downright modern tip–waist–tail dimensions (84–69–76 millimeters). Interestingly, the dimensions of "modern" telemark skis have only recently caught up to the standards Norheim developed more than a century ago.

Here comes the really interesting part. Besides developing the telemark turn, Norheim was the first to demonstrate—at a major competition in Christiania in 1867—a parallel swerve of the skis that made it possible to stop quickly or to turn on icy slopes. In the early 1900s, when a commission was established to document the sport's history, the group labeled Norheim's parallel turn the Christiania Turn. The Christiania Turn (you may know this as the stem christie or the christiana swing) was the stepping-stone to today's parallel turn. Let me make this clear: The single most important figure in telemarking history was also the inventor of the parallel turn and therefore the founding father of alpine skiing. Norheim was *way* ahead of his time.

In the late 1800s a few Telemark locals introduced the Norwegian ski sport to Austria, where it was received enthusiastically. Gradually, Austrian ski schools contributed their own innovations to the sport. Most of the early competitions were still won by Norwegians, however, because they involved cross-country skiing, downhill descents, and jumping. Central European skis and techniques were better suited to steep alpine terrain.

By 1920 most skiers were using christiania-style turns because these proved faster. It was around this time that attitudes, interests, and equipment really diverged. The Norwegians didn't endorse either races emphasizing turning and downhill alone, or the heavier gear used in such competitions. Both seemed too specialized and didn't help in the development of a well-rounded skier. Cross-country, jumping, and slaloming, all on the same gear—that was the Norwegian idea of a complete skier.

The Swiss and Austrians, meanwhile, were developing gear and technique suited to the Alps. Here, people got used to the control that a fixed-heel system afforded. Still, something had to be done to facilitate skiing in the backcountry. In the 1950s somebody combined the control of the alpine skiing style with, when needed, the convenience of a free-lifting heel. It was called an "alpine-touring" (or randonnee) binding, and it became an immediate success.

Initially, alpine-touring gear was considerably heavier and sturdier than telemark gear. This was just fine, because a certain amount of mass translates power better and deflects less. In short, heavier gear worked better than featherweight equipment on the crusty, sun-cupped, windswept steeps of the high Alps.

So where does all this background leave us in the debate over whether we should telemark or alpine tour? Should we free or fix the heel? I believe that in the United States, telemarkers have put too much effort into creating a new identity for their sport. Telemarking itself became something of a religion rather than the means (or the tools) to an end: the backcountry. Telemark gear handles a lot of terrain deftly, but it isn't the best choice for every job. The same is true for alpine-touring gear.

Traditionally, telemark gear was lighter (better for distance) but offered less control in steep terrain and difficult snows than alpine-touring gear. That has all changed recently with the introduction of performance-oriented telemark equipment (pounds heavier) and slimmed-down alpine-touring rigs (pounds

*Tour 29, The Forbidden Tour*

**Don Denton approaching Camp 1 on Quien Sabe
Glacier; Johannisberg Mountain is in the background.**

*Photo by Martin Volken*

lighter). Today the light end of the alpine-touring spectrum weighs less than the gear many modern telemarkers tote into the backcountry. Skiers with a down-hill-skiing background, therefore, will be better served by alpine-touring gear—they can use techniques they're familiar with and execute a better turn for severe terrain (parallel turn), but they won't pay a weight penalty. Meanwhile, backcountry skiers who don't intend to tackle severe slopes may find light- to medium-weight telemark gear much more to their liking.

Rather than letting "religious" friends talk you into one system or the other just because they use it, gather information by asking several people the same questions. Consider the terrain, your skiing background, and your goals. And before you invest, consider renting both systems several times to see what feels right for you.

But in the end, don't get too hung up about which system you embrace. Let's take the late Allan Bard's words to heart: "The tool is up to you. It's all skiing."

# From the Lift to the Backcountry

Getting into the backcountry on skis is growing more and more popular. Just look at the recent ski movies or the spectacular photos in the ski magazines. Interestingly, I've noticed that many of the featured ski models aren't using ski-touring equipment. They seem to be somewhere way out there (and some-times they are), but how did they get there?

I conclude that many of these "backcountry" shots were taken near a ski area boundary—if not actually within the boundary. As many of these powder- and tree-skiing lovers get more familiar with the ungroomed terrain, they'll start exploring farther from lift-accessed areas. And unless they're among the few who can afford $500 per day for the wildest ski lift available, they'll sooner or later start looking at some kind of touring gear.

Here the "cardiovascular selection" begins. Some people are very certain that gravity is there to be taken advantage of and not to be fought against. Many people leave it at that. Other folks don't mind walking uphill for several hours in order to ski down some windblown slope for a few minutes, and after-ward convincing themselves that it was worth it. I'm part of the latter group and am proud to say that I can show many people every year that there's a lot more to skiing than the actual downhill portion.

As soon as people with good judgment start considering this new segment of the ski sport, they realize that they might be rather ill prepared for the back-country. This starts with orienteering (no neatly color-coded signs out there); then the snow seems more difficult, snow stability is unpredictable, weather and time are factors, and if something does go wrong, you're on your own. If you decide to get into alpine touring or even ski mountaineering, the topic gets even more involved. All this is part of the beauty of this sport, but it takes some preparation.

Many very good skiers are completely unfamiliar with the workings of a winter environment. Our young hot-dog skiers look up to people like John

Treeman, the Egan brothers, and Scott Schmidt. It's often overlooked that these professional extremists do their homework. They usually have a good idea what they're getting into. The few I've met struck me as individuals with a very good sense of judgment who aren't afraid to say no if the conditions are not right.

But how do you even know if the conditions are right? *Get some experience.* The transition phase is important, exciting—and dangerous. You have to get out there if you want to get miles under your skis and skins, but your lack of experience makes you a prime candidate to get into trouble. Try to educate yourself, seek out clubs or experienced individuals, and consider hiring a guide. I *don't* recommend the "I'm just gonna go for it" attitude in the backcountry.

Most of my students come out of my ski touring course excited and thoughtful at the same time. There's a lot to be learned when you decide to make your own up- or downhill tracks. But that's also what will take skiing to a new dimension for you.

# Equipment for the Backcountry Skier

Generally speaking, I believe backcountry users of all persuasions overpack. For several years I've worked on optimizing my climbing, mountaineering, and ski-touring loads. Initially I carried way too much gear. After a little experience I tried carrying as little as possible. Now, following some chilly nights, some hungry days, and some luck, I believe the optimal pack lies between the extremes.

That happy middle ground is difficult to pinpoint, of course, because so much depends on individual skills and comfort levels. I do believe certain items are essential for safe ski touring and ski mountaineering, and in the following list I've collected threesomes that logically fit together. The intent of the threesomes is to make you an efficient, thorough packer—packing each item will remind you to bring two counterparts. This will reduce the likelihood of forgetting important safety equipment.

For backcountry skiing and ski touring, I've put together a three-by-nine list. Ski mountaineering demands more gear and has two extra trios of equipment to pack.

### Backcountry-Skiing and Ski-Touring Equipment Checklist

- Skis, boots, poles
- Maps, compass, altimeter
- Shovel, probe, transceiver
- Skins, ski crampons, repair kit
- Food, drink, extra layer of clothing
- Bivi bag, first-aid kit, cell phone
- Underlayer, midlayer, outer layer
- Hat, glove, goggles
- Sunglasses, sunscreen, sun hat

### Additional Equipment for Ski Mountaineering

- Harness, ice ax, crampons
- Rope, ice screws, rescue gear kit

Not all items on the three-by-nine list (for instance, ski crampons, goggles, sun hat, extra layers) are needed for every tour. When in doubt, however, opt for more gear rather than less—a few extra pounds won't spoil a day trip.

I include a cell phone in my basic kit. Cell phones in the backcountry are controversial, and some folks are dead-set against them. I don't carry a cell phone so I can call my friends from the summit. I carry one because in an emergency, it may save the lives of my friends and students.

# Tour Planning
## Planning Considerations

Several years ago Werner Munter, the renowned Swiss Mountain Guide and avalanche expert, developed guidelines for tour preparation. I've adapted them with his permission. I personally use them in every aspect of my guiding profession. The guidelines are a tool, and like any other tool you'll learn to use them better over time. I am probably more impressed with this simple summary of tour preparation right now than I was several years ago.

Planning for a backcountry tour starts with regional planning you should do before the trip, and continues while you're in the field. Following are key considerations for tour planning.

## Regional Planning at Home

- Evaluate weather and snow conditions. Obtain information about conditions from the avalanche forecast (206–526–6677) and local weather forecast (206–526–6087). Both forecasts are also available on-line at www.seawfo. noaa.gov/nwac.html.
- Determine your basic route. Use topographic maps, time calculations, guidebooks, and information from local experts.
- Evaluate the personnel and gear. How strong is the weakest participant? How well is the group equipped?

## Local Planning: Evaluating the Tour in the Field

- Observe the snow conditions. Be especially aware of avalanche-risk factors, such as spontaneous releases, settling sounds, critical precipitation amounts, wind transport, and cornices.
- Watch the weather. Keep track of changing visibility, temperature, wind, wind direction, radiation, and cloud cover.
- Observe the terrain: steepness, exposure, ridge location and orientation, underlying vegetation, and objective hazards.

## *Zonal Planning: Evaluating a Particular Slope*

- Observe the steepness of the slope. It's important to consider the *steepest* part of the slope—don't rely on averages.
- Is the new snow loose or consolidated? Simple shovel tests are very helpful here.
- Is there a glide layer?

These guidelines are only as good as the information you gather and your skill in interpreting it. Work hard to develop good sources of information and at applying brainpower to the data.

I'd like to stress again a point I made above. Whether you're digging a hasty pit, a regular pit, or a Rutsch block, or ski-cutting a slope for zonal evaluation, *it is crucial to translate your results to the steepest part of the slope*. And remember that snow pits don't deliver conclusive results. In all my days of guiding, I have yet to dig an elaborate pit; but I have turned around (or altered plans) many times due to questionable snow stability. In a real-world situation, you probably will have noted several clues pointing toward questionable stability by the time you think about digging a big pit.

There are many quick and elegant ways of staying in tune with snow stability, such as ski-cutting, snow sound, hasty pits, pole compression tests, and shovel shear tests. These tests can be conducted many times a day; some continue over the course of the touring day. They'll provide you with many clues.

# Time Calculations

Just about every experienced mountaineer can tell you about a trip whose time estimates were grossly inadequate. On spring ski tours this problem is compounded by the daily avalanche cycle (see below), so keep this cycle in mind when planning your tour.

When calculating the time required for a tour, consider these three main components:

**1.** Amount of vertical uphill

**2.** Amount of vertical downhill

**3.** Amount of horizontal distance

Generally, I don't apply formulas to a mountain setting, but the following one has proven surprisingly accurate. I use it regularly for my tour planning.

**1.** Convert the amount of uphill vertical into units such that 300 feet of vertical gain represents 1 unit.

**2.** Convert the amount of downhill vertical into units such that 300 feet of vertical loss represents 1 unit.

*Tour 29, The Forbidden Tour, Day 4*
**Freddie Grossniklaus and Jeff Hansell
descending off El Dorado.**

*Photo by Scott Schell*

**3.** Convert the amount of horizontal distance into units such that 1 kilometer (or 0.6 mile) represents 1 unit.

**Example:** Your ascent has a (one-way) horizontal distance of 6 kilometers (3.7 miles) and involves 3,000 vertical feet of climbing; your descent has the same 6 kilometers of horizontal distance and a 3,000-vertical-foot drop. This tour's ascent has 16 units, and its descent has 16 units.

**Converting these units into time:**

**1.** For the ascent: Divide your uphill units by 4. The result equals your climbing time in hours (4 hours in our example). This factor of 4 results from the experience that 4 kilometers per hour is a good average distance to be covered on flat terrain. The uphill vertical gets factored in by adding units to the total before converting those units into time.

**2.** For the descent: Divide the downhill units by 10. The result equals your descent time in hours (1.6 hours in our example). The factor of 10 comes from the experience that 10 kilometers per hour is a good average distance to be covered on skis when in downhill mode.

**3.** Total time: Add the two times (5.6 hours in our example).

This time calculation accounts for short breaks but not for long ones such as an extended lunch.

**Very important:** This time calculation assumes average touring conditions, and that skiers are in good shape and possess average touring abilities. Add or subtract time accordingly. With a little practice, you'll come to appreciate this formula. A few years ago I was planning an ambitious tour. After conducting a fairly accurate time calculation, I discovered that I would have to traverse several 35- to 40-degree south-facing slopes at 2:30 P.M. instead of noon, as I'd hoped. This changed my plans for that day in May.

# The Seasonal-Stability Dial

The majority of avalanches trapping skiers occur on aspects ranging from north-northwest to northeast. The wind deposits from our prevailing westerlies and the slower settling of northern slopes create dangerous winter conditions for skiers. Ironically, wintertime skiing is best on these northern aspects for the same reasons. This means heli-skiing companies and backcountry skiers alike are often making tricky judgment calls.

In midwinter skiing is generally safer on other aspects, and safety-conscious skiers are wise to avoid northern slopes—especially those with a pitch between 28 and 45 degrees. During this time, slopes with southerly aspects consolidate faster and are usually more stable.

As the season progresses, the stability dial moves counterclockwise. The sun gets more powerful and initiates a melt-freeze cycle that makes touring and skiing on the previously stable southerly slopes trickier—these slopes lose stability as the day progresses, then stabilize at night as they refreeze. Meanwhile, the previously unstable northerly aspects are finally consolidating due to the increased sunshine and warmth and often offer safe skiing at this point.

When does the snowpack switch from winter to spring conditions? Following the weather and avalanche forecasts over the course of the winter will help you answer this question, but it's a difficult one. The transition is also a tricky time to ski and the period, statistically, when the most avalanche fatalities occur. During this transition, avalanche danger is often considered moderate and clues are hard to read. New hazards are just forming on southern slopes while old hazards may still linger on the northern slopes.

At some point in spring, the melt-freeze cycle changes to a melt-a-lot-freeze-a-little cycle. This warm, spring mountain weather initiates the so-called climax cycle. At this point the snowpack has gone through several melt-freeze cycles and may freeze only very superficially during the night, or not at all. The wet snowpack drains moisture down to the next lower gliding layer. This is usually a rain crust or a rock slab where water has been flowing for quite some time. At some point the pull of gravity exceeds the basal cohesion and very large, wet avalanches may occur. These avalanches don't necessarily follow a daily cycle, because the snowpack doesn't regain a lot of strength at night.

After this the snowpack becomes quite stable, and skiing in high alpine regions can be very good. This is the time (mid- to late June) when golfers should ask themselves whether they should pack away the clubs and pull out the skis.

**Important:** Don't let this be the only thing you read about avalanche cycles—applying general rules to specific situations may do you more harm than good. Remember that every season has its avalanche dangers. Also, this basic seasonal-stability cycle is constantly influenced by inconsistencies in the weather. You must combine this basic information with more detailed information pertinent to the particular weather cycle and area.

# The Unavoidable Rating System

I spent a long time debating whether a rating system would be useful in this book. After a good amount of thought, I had to conclude that it serves a good purpose.

The intent of this rating system is not to categorize ski tourers into certain ability levels, but rather to be an effective tool in the process of tour preparation and planning.

It seems very important to me that people make distinctions among backcountry skiing, alpine ski touring, and ski mountaineering.

Pure *backcountry skiing* is very often the first step away from the lift. A lot of this skiing takes place below or around timberline and doesn't involve any glacier travel or mixed alpine travel. Backcountry skiing is the least committing form of the sport.

*Alpine ski touring* is a more committing form of backcountry skiing. Usually the tours are more remote, involve more map and compass skills, and in general start to take on a more alpine flavor (much of the skiing may take place above timberline).

The distinction between a backcountry ski tour and an alpine ski tour is very often fluid and may even be different on the same tour, depending on time of the year, weather, snow and route conditions, and so on. Use your judgment!

*Ski mountaineering* may and most likely will involve glacier travel, and can involve elements from the world of mixed mountaineering—roped travel, crevasse rescue skills, or basic ridge, rock, and ice climbing.

Here are the elements that I find crucial when judging the difficulty of a tour:

- Length of the tour
- Distance from civilization
- Difficulty of the terrain
- How committing the tour is
- Skiing ability and physical fitness required
- Whether the area is avalanche prone
- Average tour elevation (below or above timberline)
- Glacier travel
- Mixed mountaineering elements

I divided the described tours into five grades of difficulty:

**Grade I.** This tour certainly is no longer than a few hours, is close to civilization, and doesn't involve difficult terrain. Tour break-off points are plentiful, or the tour is so short that you can simply turn around. The skiing isn't demanding. Objective avalanche hazards are generally low. The tour doesn't involve any alpine ski-touring or ski-mountaining elements.

**Grade II.** This is still a shorter tour but may involve one or two of the elements mentioned above as more committing—steeper skiing or more avalanche-prone terrain. It might be right on the cusp of being considered an alpine ski tour, depending on conditions. For this reason you need to take this tour quite seriously and be well prepared.

**Grade III.** This could be an overnight trip whose elements are all fairly moderate. It could also be a day trip with some of the elements packaged in a very advanced form: for example, a ski tour that's only about 6 hours long but involves a committing drop into a 45-degree couloir and terrain that's very difficult to assess in terms of avalanche danger. Remember that a Grade III trip can turn very serious in bad weather or changing snow conditions.

**Grade IV.** This is an alpine ski tour or a ski-mountaineering trip that's surely an overnight and contains several of the elements on an advanced level. Superior physical fitness and skiing ability are prerequisites. Solid ski-touring experience is highly recommended.

**Grade V.** This is a multiday ski-touring adventure with a serious route commitment; breaking off during the tour might open up a whole new set of problems. Prior mountaineering experience is highly recommended; skiing ability and physical fitness levels must be high; and several years of general ski-touring experience is a must.

Keep in mind that rating systems are misleading. Things change very quickly in the mountains, and moderate tours can become difficult and dangerous very suddenly. Lack of tour-planning ability has cost many people their lives in the mountains. A recent longitudinal study in Switzerland has shown that more than 50 percent of the ski-touring fatalities of the last 10 years could have been prevented with solid tour preparation. Please consider this rating system as just one of the elements that will help you be properly prepared before you leave home.

## How to Use This Guide

This book should help your tour planning at home and help guide you out in the field. *Help* is the operative word. The book won't supply every detail; it's up to you to fill in what's missing. Furthermore, this guide cannot guarantee your safety—you must evaluate whether your abilities and the conditions of the day allow safe passage. Finally, while I've striven for accuracy, I'm not foolish enough to believe every detail is right—you shouldn't be so foolish either.

All of this means that your safety depends on you. You will notice many warnings like these: *Be careful; use your judgment; you have to feel good about it; assess the situation* . . . There are no absolutes in the mountains. Be conservative when judging your abilities, prepare your tours carefully, question what I've written, and, once you're out on a tour, be willing to turn around.

The detailed information at the beginning of each tour will give you valuable information for deciding whether or not a particular tour is right for you. This data includes:

**Tour distance:** Distances are listed in kilometers because the map grids are sectioned off in square kilometers. This should help you visualize the distances mentioned. Also, all distances are approximate, because it's very hard to calculate switchbacks. You'll find differences between the distances indicated on the quick-info charts and the ones on the elevation profiles. Those on the elevation profiles are on horizontal distance only.

**Tour time:** Time calculations indicate traveling time for ski tourers with adequate experience and conditioning for the tour. The calculations also assume average snow and weather conditions. An inexperienced skier tackling a hard tour might take twice the indicated time, while a superfit, experienced skier might require considerably less time than is listed. Conditions and weather can easily shut you down for several days on a longer tour—factor this into your planning.

**Vertical gain/loss:** Vertical gain and loss have been indicated in feet because contour lines are represented in 40-foot intervals.

**Difficulty rating:** See The Unavoidable Rating System on page 13.

**Best season:** I've suggested best seasons for each tour based on average conditions in average snow years.

**Starting elevation/high point:** The starting elevation is not always the low point of the tour.

**Gear required:** Please refer to Equipment for the Backcountry Skier on page 8.

**Required fitness and skiing ability:** Fitness and ability levels should be taken seriously. Because all the tours described will be harder in bad weather or snow conditions, be conservative when judging your abilities.

**Maps needed:** The topographic maps in this book are for reference only and are not substitutes for U.S. Geological Survey (USGS) quadrangles. This is especially true for longer tours, where map scales were increased to illustrate the entire tour.

**Elevation profiles:** Note that the distance figures listed on the elevation profiles don't take switchbacks into account. Vertical gain and loss figures on the elevation profiles are also approximate. Finally, the profiles don't always show the complete tour—several profiles stop where the descent meets the ascent route.

# Day Tours
## 1-21

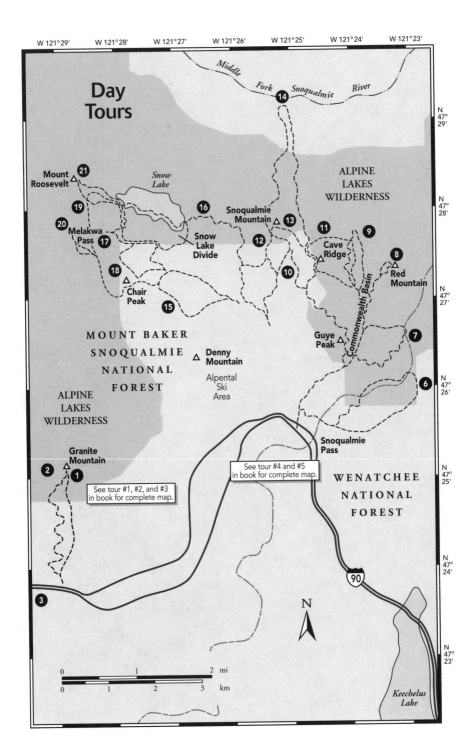

# Day Tours

W 121° 29'  W 121° 28'  W 121° 27'  W 121° 26'  W 121° 25'  W 121° 24'  W 121° 23'

*Middle Fork Snoqualmie River*

**14**

Snow Lake

**21** Mount Roosevelt △

ALPINE LAKES WILDERNESS

**19**

**16**

Snoqualmie Mountain △ **13**

**11**

**9**

**20** **17** Melakwa Pass

Snow Lake Divide

**12**

Cave Ridge

**8** △ Red Mountain

**18** △ Chair Peak

**10**

Commonwealth Basin

**15**

MOUNT BAKER SNOQUALMIE NATIONAL FOREST

△ Denny Mountain

Guye Peak △

**7**

ALPINE LAKES WILDERNESS

Alpental Ski Area

**6**

Snoqualmie Pass

WENATCHEE NATIONAL FOREST

Granite Mountain

**2** △ **1**

See tour #4 and #5 in book for complete map.

See tour #1, #2, and #3 in book for complete map.

**3**

N 47° 29'

N 47° 28'

N 47° 27'

N 47° 26'

N 47° 25'

N 47° 24'

N 47° 23'

90

N

0        1        2 mi
0    1    2    3 km

*Keechelus Lake*

# Day Tours

# Granite Mountain

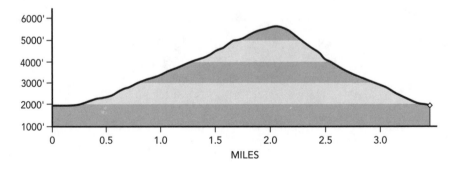

**Tour distance:** 8 km (5 miles)

**Tour time:** 5 to 6 hours

**Vertical gain/loss:** 3,749 feet/3,749 feet

**Difficulty rating:** Grade II-plus

**Best season:** January through April

**Starting elevation/high point:** 1,880 feet/5,629 feet

**Gear required:** Standard ski-touring equipment

**Required fitness and skiing ability:** Good physical fitness and advanced skiing ability

**Map needed:** Snoqualmie Pass

Granite Mountain is a classic moderate ski tour in the Snoqualmie Valley. Access doesn't get any better, the vertical is quite respectable, the skiing can be really good, and the summit views are extraordinary. If it's important to you to ski maximum vertical, it would be worthwhile to pay attention to the snow level here, due to the low starting elevation.

**Approach:** From Interstate 90 take the Denny Creek exit west of Snoqualmie Pass. After exiting drive to the north side of the freeway. At the T intersection go west as far as you can and then park your vehicle. Start your tour here. You're now exactly south of the summit and 200 to 300 meters (600 to 900 feet) west of the obvious drainage—which has gotten hikers and tourers into trouble before.

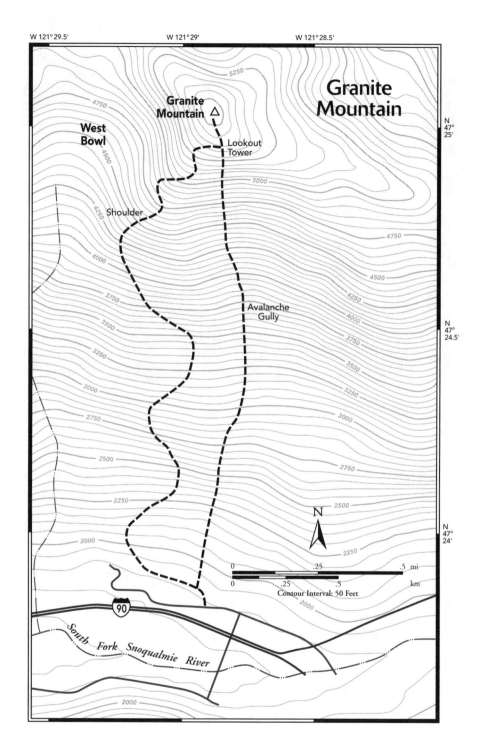

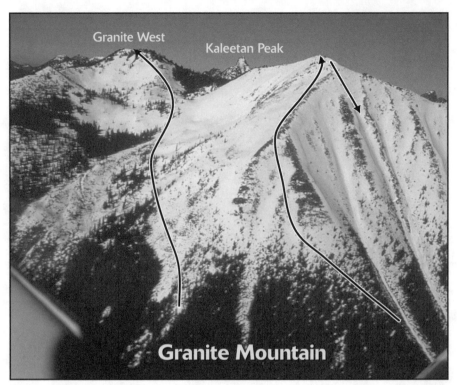

Granite Mountain from south. PHOTO BY MARTIN VOLKEN

The upper half of Granite Mountain's south face consists of a shallow but broad bowl that gets an enormous amount of wind-deposited snow. In spring you can see spectacular amounts of climax-slide debris while driving past on I–90. The hiking trail goes right through the heart of the slide path, and that might have lured ski tourers into the area in the past. A very direct and safe way to the upper reaches is to tour north through the forest from the road-head. At around 3,600 feet you'll break out of the trees. You're still south of the summit and between the south face drainage and a bigger drainage that originates in the bowl west of the summit (1.5 hours to here). From here tour north-northwest to gain the bottom of a broad shoulder at 4,200 feet. This shoulder divides the broad south face from the west bowl and is often wind scoured. You should be able to find a safe way up the shoulder in just about any condition. The western edge of the shoulder will give you great views into the bowl west of the summit, which can provide fantastic skiing down to 4,000 feet.

Tour up the shoulder in a northeasterly direction to the summit of Granite Mountain (5,629 feet; 3.5 hours to here). For the descent you can of course reverse your ascent track; this should be a safe way down, even in questionable conditions. You can also ski down the east ridge to about 4,500 feet and then ski south and southwest off the ridge from there. You'll reach your car easily (4 to 5 hours to here). If the conditions allow for steeper skiing, the west bowl can offer some incredible turns down to 4,000 feet. The entrance into the bowl is steep and requires good assessment, but the aspect of the bowl shelters the snow quite nicely and may make a couple of laps a must. From the bottom of the bowl at 4,000 feet, ski southeast and regain your ascent track. If you're spring skiing and are a so-called dawn-patrol skier, you may find incredible corn snow down the south face. As I've mentioned, this slope is avalanche prone and can prove dangerous. Certainly try to stay ahead of the sun here. If you decide to go for the south slope option, you should be able to ski down the fall line from the summit for about 3,000 feet. Then ski out of the drainage in a southwesterly direction through the forest and back to your car (4.5 to 5 hours for this option).

# Granite West

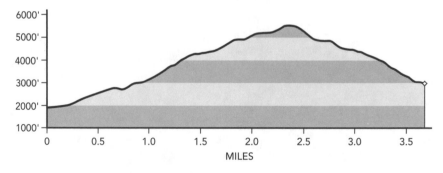

**Tour distance:** 7.5 km (4.7 miles)

**Tour time:** 4 to 6 hours

**Vertical gain/loss:** 3,280 feet/3,280 feet

**Difficulty rating:** Grade II-plus

**Best season:** January through April

**Starting elevation/high point:** 1,880 feet/5,160 feet

**Gear required:** Standard ski-touring gear

**Required fitness and skiing ability:** Average physical fitness and intermediate skiing ability

**Maps needed:** Snoqualmie Pass; Bandera for optional descents

This short, simple tour combines enjoyable subalpine tree skiing with spectacular views of the west cirque of Granite Mountain. The described tour can be done in most conditions, making it ideal in adverse weather. Additional descent options are available in better conditions by continuing along the ridge to the summit of Peak 5566. Go when the snow line is low if you want to use your skis the entire way; otherwise, pack your skis to reach the snow line. Route information for this tour has been provided by American Mountain Guides Association ski-mountaineering guide Ben Haskell.

**Approach:** From Interstate 90 take the Denny Creek exit west of Snoqualmie Pass. After exiting drive to the north side of the freeway. At the T intersection go west as far as you can and then park your vehicle. Start your tour here.

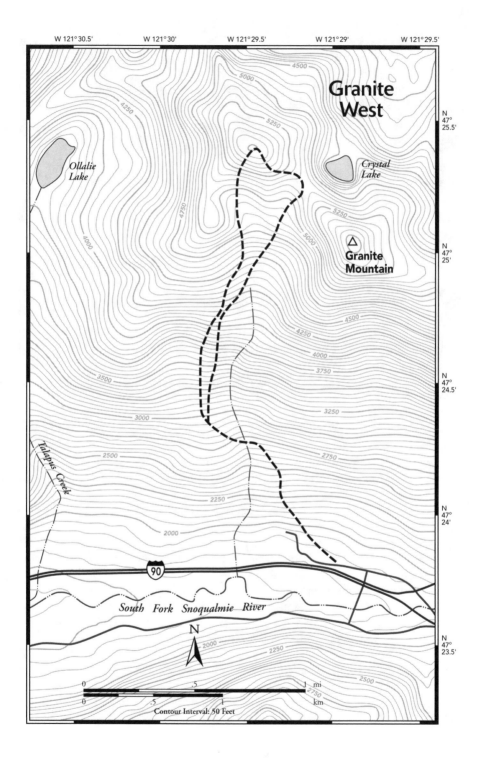

Granite
West

Ollalie
Lake

Crystal
Lake

△
Granite
Mountain

Talapus Creek

90

South Fork Snoqualmie River

N

| 0 | | .5 | | 1 mi |

| 0 | .5 | | 1 | km |

Contour Interval: 50 Feet

W 121° 30.5'    W 121° 30'    W 121° 29.5'    W 121° 29'    W 121° 29.5'

N 47° 25.5'
N 47° 25'
N 47° 24.5'
N 47° 24'
N 47° 23.5'

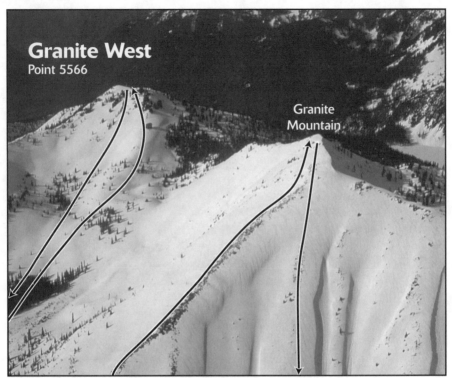

Granite Mountain and Granite West (Point 5566) from southeast. PHOTO BY SCOTT SCHELL

Tour in a northwesterly direction from the parking lot for about 1 km (0.6 mile) to the major creek drainage that descends from the western flanks of Granite Mountain. Cross the creek just below 2,800 feet (about 1 hour to here). In most conditions the creek crossing can more easily be reached by following the well-defined Pratt Lake Trail. After crossing the creek, the trail switchbacks up to 2,880 feet. Head north at this point on the shallow ridge that parallels the creek. A steep and brushy section starting at around 3,600 feet leads to more open timber at around 4,000 feet (about 2 to 2.5 hours to here). Continue north to the ridge crest at 5,160 feet for views into the spectacular west cirque of Granite Mountain (about 3.5 hours to here). Descend your ascent route, being careful not to trend east into the drainage itself, which is subject to avalanches from the entire cirque (4.5 to 6 hours to here).

In stable conditions the ridge can be followed to the summit of Peak 5566 (about 4 hours to here). Then you can ski the west ridge of the peak back down to the Pratt Lake Trail above Ollalie Lake (this trail isn't normally visible in deep snow). Return to the parking lot by contouring in a southeasterly direction starting near 3,800 feet.

# McClellum Butte North Couloir

**Tour distance:** 6 km (3.7 miles)

**Tour time:** 6 to 8 hours

**Vertical gain/loss:** 3,062 feet/3,062 feet

**Difficulty rating:** Grade IV (Grade IV+ if you attempt the summit)

**Best season:** January through April

**Starting elevation/high point:** About 2,100 feet/5,162 feet

**Gear required:** Standard ski-touring gear plus rope, harness, crampons, some rock protection, helmet

**Required fitness and skiing ability:** Very good physical fitness and excellent skiing ability. Some prior mountaineering experience is recommended.

**Map needed:** Bandera Mountain

This couloir is hard to resist. It's more a steep ski descent than an actual ski tour. You'll easily see your objective from Interstate 90 at around milepost 40 on the south side of the freeway. The line is pure, steep (50 degrees at the top), and topped off with a summit block that can put a bit of mountaineering flavor into your outing. The summit should be attempted only by those with prior mountaineering experience. Solid skiing and snow-safety judgment skills are a prerequisite for the descent of the couloir.

**Approach:** Drive I–90 to eastbound exit 38. Turn right at the stop sign and fol-

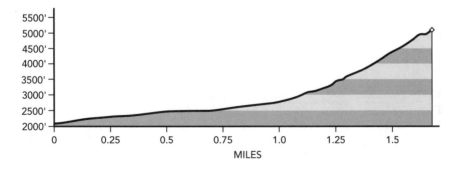

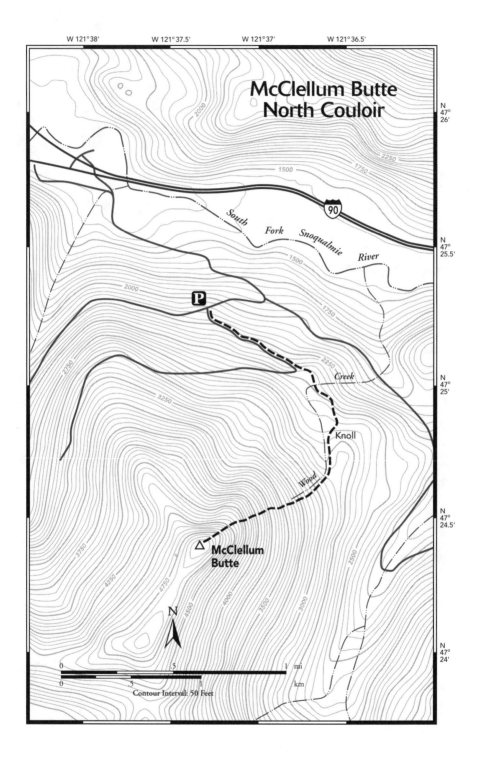

McClellum Butte
North Couloir

W 121°38'    W 121°37.5'    W 121°37'    W 121°36.5'

N 47° 26'
N 47° 25.5'
N 47° 25'
N 47° 24.5'
N 47° 24'

South Fork Snoqualmie River

90

Creek

Knoll

Wood

McClellum
Butte

N

0        .5        1 mi
0        .5        1 km

Contour Interval: 50 Feet

**McClellum Butte
North Couloir**

low this road to the point where it merges with the interstate again. Here at 1,350 feet a dirt road goes off to your right. Follow this road across the Iron Horse Trail (1,640 feet). Continue up to 1,880 feet. Here another dirt road turns off to your right. Follow this road until it switchbacks at 2,100 feet. This is a good place to park unless the road is still snow-free; in that case continue up the road to a switchback at 2,480 feet.

From the switchback at 2,100 feet, start walking or touring up the old logging road in a southeasterly direction to the switchback at 2,480 feet. There's a more primitive logging road that continues in the same direction for another 0.5 kilometer (0.3 mile) to 2,800 feet (about 1 hour to here).

This point—at 2,800 feet and at the end of the old logging road—is a key spot. You're now right under your objective. Tour up the slope in a south-southwesterly direction to about 3,100 feet, leaving a knoll on your left. At this point you'll be breaking out of the trees.

Absolutely abandon the tour here if you have any doubt about snow stability. Consider that many of this spot's slides are caused by debris falling into the couloir.

From here simply follow the Wood Creek drainage (that's what this couloir effectively is) up to the summit block (5,100 feet; about 3 to 4 hours to here). You might have to use crampons. The shoulder on the left-hand side of the couloir makes an excellent high point for the tour if you don't want to tackle the summit block via its short but sporty northeast ridge.

Tackling the summit block will require you to have rope, harness, and some basic rock protection with you. You should count on another hour from your ski depot at 5,100 feet to the summit and back.

To descend, reverse your tracks back to the ski depot and then enjoy the ski descent.

# Mount Catherine

**Tour distance:** 8 km (5 miles)

**Tour time:** 4 to 6 hours

**Vertical gain/loss:** 2,500 feet/2,500 feet

**Difficulty rating:** Grade II-plus

**Best season:** January through April

**Starting elevation/high point:** 2,600 feet/5,052 feet

**Gear required:** Standard ski-touring equipment

**Required fitness and skiing ability:** Good physical fitness and advanced skiing ability

**Map needed:** Snoqualmie Pass

Mount Catherine is a surprising tour. I was looking for a very simple noncommitting outing. What I found was a surprising amount of vertical and a long ski descent in fairly steep old-growth forest. The generally northerly aspect here in the forest shelters the snow more than most tours in the area. The summit views toward the Gold Creek drainage are spectacular.

**Approach:** Drive Interstate 90 to exit 53 and proceed to the main parking lot of the Hyak Ski Area at 2,600 feet.
　　Start touring up the ski area to the top of the smaller lift (tourer's right). Here (2,920 feet) turn right and tour up the cat track for about 300 meters (900 feet). The cat track merges with a ski run here. Turn left (south-southwest) and tour up the run to a broad col at 3,400 feet (about 1 hour to here). Now fol-

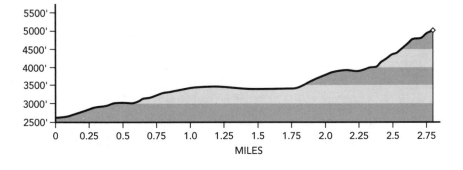

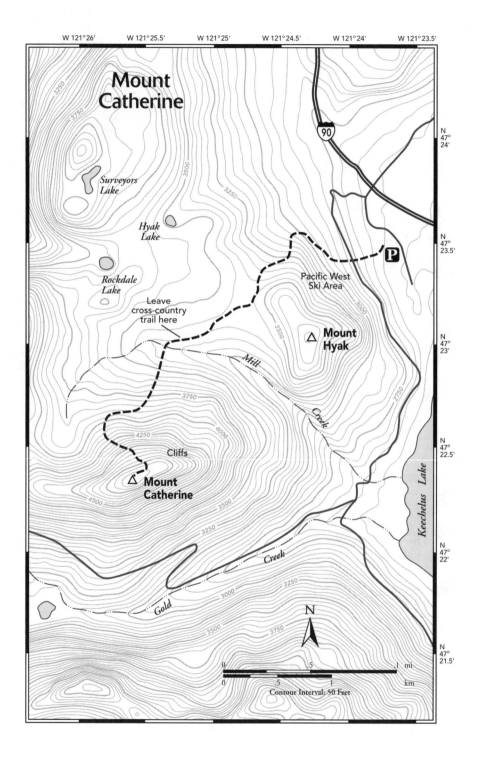

low the cross-country trail in a southwesterly direction to a bridge (about 3,350 feet; 1.5 hours to here).

Leave the cross-country trail and tour in a southerly direction through logged terrain to 3,600 feet. You'll be able to enter old-growth forest on your right now. At around 3,950 feet you'll come to a flatter area in the forest with very steep terrain right above you. It's important to stay at this elevation for about 300 meters (900 feet) while touring west. Do so until you're at the broad northwest-facing shoulder that leads right to the summit. Follow the shoulder to the top. This description sounds easy, but the terrain isn't as obvious in the forest (5,052 feet; about 3.5 hours to here).

To descend, reverse your ascent track (2,600 feet; about 5 hours to here).

*Tour 4*
**Peter Avolio coming off Mt. Catherine's summit.**

*Photo by Martin Volken*

# Mount Hyak

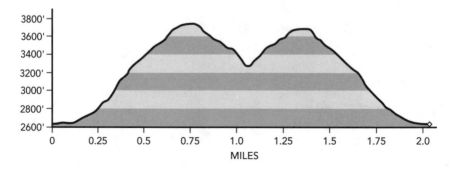

**Tour distance:** 3.5 km (2.1 miles)

**Tour time:** 2 to 3 hours

**Vertical gain/loss:** 1,645 feet/1,645 feet

**Difficulty rating:** Grade I

**Best season:** December through April

**Starting elevation/high point:** 2,600 feet/3,745 feet

**Gear required:** Standard ski-touring equipment

**Required fitness and skiing ability:** Good fitness and intermediate skiing ability

**Map needed:** Snoqualmie Pass

Mount Hyak is located just barely east of the Hyak Ski Area and makes for an excellent little tour for the absolute novice. You need neither prior touring experience, mountain sense, map-reading skills, avalanche safety knowledge, nor great physical endurance. You should have but one objective: to get acquainted with your gear. The Hyak Ski Area is frequently closed during the week and in early winter, so you can simply tour up the ski slopes during these times.

**Approach:** Drive Interstate 90 to exit 53 and proceed to the main parking lot of the Hyak Ski Area at 2,600 feet.

From the parking lot (2,600 feet), start touring up the obvious slope of the ski area. Please don't try this if the ski area is open! Reach the top of the Hyak Ski Area at 3,650 feet (about 1 hour to here), then proceed in a southeasterly

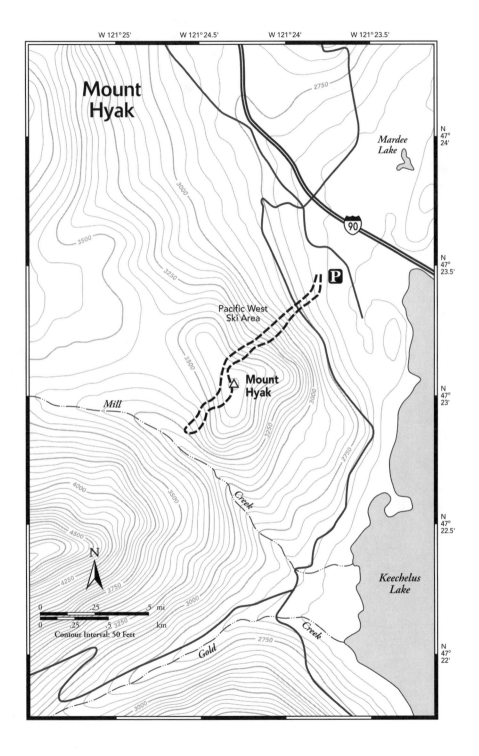

direction to the top of Mount Hyak (3,745 feet; about 1.25 hours to here).

If conditions are good, you can ski off the other side in a southwesterly direction into the Mill Creek Valley to about 3,200 feet (about 1.5 hours to here).

Return to your car via your ascent and descent track (about 2.5 hours to here).

# Kendall Stump

**Tour distance:** 4 to 5 km (2.5 to 3.1 miles)

**Tour time:** 3 to 4 hours

**Vertical gain/loss:** 2,020 feet/2,020 feet

**Difficulty rating:** Grade I

**Best season:** December through May

**Starting elevation/high point:** 2,980 feet/5,000 feet

**Gear required:** Standard ski-touring equipment

**Required fitness and skiing ability:** Good physical fitness and intermediate skiing ability

**Map needed:** Snoqualmie Pass

The hill directly north east of Snoqualmie Pass and southeast of the Commonwealth Creek drainage provides an ideal training ground for the ski-touring novice. Don't go to Kendall Stump if you want a half day in a serene mountain wilderness. There will be noise from Interstate 90, and you'll be touring up a clear-cut for a good part of the way. Solitude isn't the point of this tour, however; instead it features moderate length, easy access, moderate avalanche potential, good skiing, and a generally low commitment grade that lets you concentrate on getting acquainted with your touring gear.

**Approach:** Reach Snoqualmie Pass via I–90 and take the west exit. Leave your vehicle in the parking lot of the Summit West Ski Area.

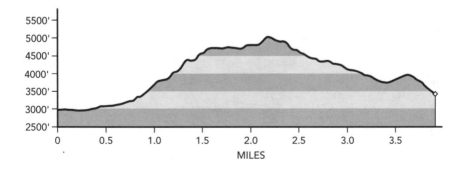

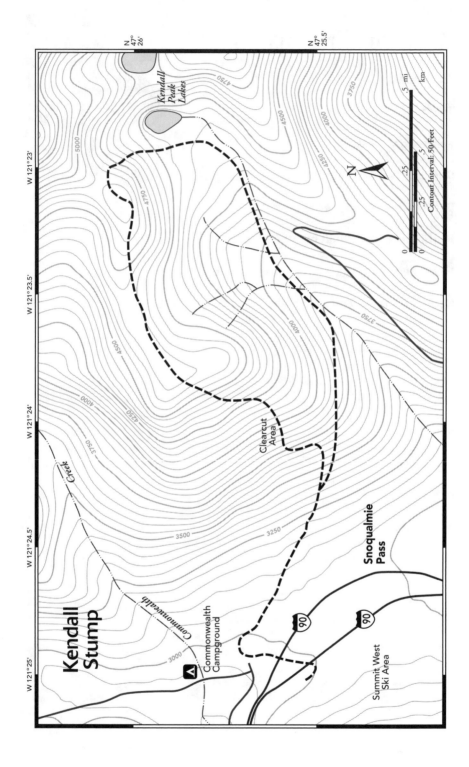

**Kendall Stump**

Kendall Peak Lakes

Creek

Commonwealth

Commonwealth Campground

Clearcut Area

Snoqualmie Pass

Summit West Ski Area

90

90

N

Contour Interval: 50 Feet

Start your tour by walking on Alpental Road to the Commonwealth turn-off. Follow up the short road to the parking area and start touring in an easterly direction for about 1 kilometer (0.6 mile). You're basically following the Pacific Crest Trail up to this point. At around 3,400 feet start touring north-northeast up the hill. You should always be able to see the freeway; don't wrap around to a more westerly aspect, as the Pacific Crest Trail does. The terrain is much steeper and somewhat cliff studded there.

At around 4,700 feet you'll pop up to the beginning of a gentle, timbered ridge that trends toward Kendall Peak (1.5 hours to here). Tour along this ridge for about 0.5 kilometer (0.3 mile) in a northeasterly direction. A pretty basin that's part of the Kendall Peak Tour (see Tour 7) will be on your left. At about 4,800 feet the ridge turns east and then northeast again until it culminates in a little bump at 5,000 feet (2 to 2.5 hours to here). This is your high point.

You have three options for the descent:

**Option 1:** Simply reverse your ascent track and return to the Commonwealth parking lot. The skiing can be very good (3 to 3.5 hours to here).

**Option 2:** Ski off your high point in a northeasterly direction to the distinct saddle at 4,900 feet. From here turn east and ski down to Kendall Lakes. Then ski out the drainage in a southwesterly direction to about 3,600 feet, and make a long descending traverse in a westerly direction toward the Commonwealth parking lot (3 to 4 hours to here).

**Option 3:** From the distinct saddle at 4,900 feet, ski down into the previously mentioned basin that leads toward Commonwealth Creek. The entrance into the basin is steep for about 200 vertical feet. From here enjoy the beautiful descent toward the western edge of this little hanging valley at about 4,200 feet. It's important to stay skier's right (north) of the drainage at this point. It's easy to get lured down too far, which will position you in steep and cliff-studded terrain. You don't want to be there if this intermediate tour is right for you. At 4,200 feet start skiing in a northwesterly direction for about 900 feet and let the gentler terrain lead you down to Commonwealth Creek.

From here (about 3,600 feet) head downstream east of the creek. At 3,400 feet turn away from the creek and ski in a more southerly direction through young timber to Commonwealth Road just west of the parking area. Then you can cover the short distance to your vehicle via the ascent route (3.5 to 4 hours to here).

# Kendall Peak, West Flank

**Tour distance:** 6 to 7 km (3.7 to 4.3 miles)

**Tour time:** 4 to 5 hours

**Vertical gain/loss:** 2,804 feet/2,804 feet

**Difficulty rating:** Grade III+

**Best season:** December through April

**Starting elevation/high point:** 2,980 feet/5,784 feet

**Gear required:** Basic ski-touring gear, rope and harness, ice ax, and 2 to 4 pieces of medium protection

**Required fitness and skiing ability:** Very good fitness and advanced skiing ability

**Map needed:** Snoqualmie Pass

Kendall Peak is a surprisingly rugged peak that can get your attention in the summit area. The ski descent demands good snow-stability assessment.

**Approach:** Reach Snoqualmie Pass via Interstate 90 and take the west exit. Leave your vehicle in the Summit West Ski Area parking lot.

Follow the parking lot access road until it turns east—just a short distance. Turn left off the road and start touring up to the Commonwealth valley. Stay generally east of the creek until you reach a flat area next to Commonwealth Creek at around 3,560 feet. This is a key spot for many of the tours described. Up until the fall of 1999, there was a log crossing possibility at the flat spot.

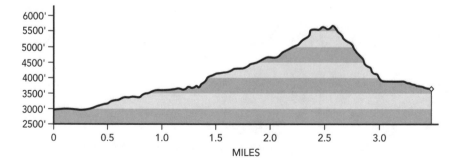

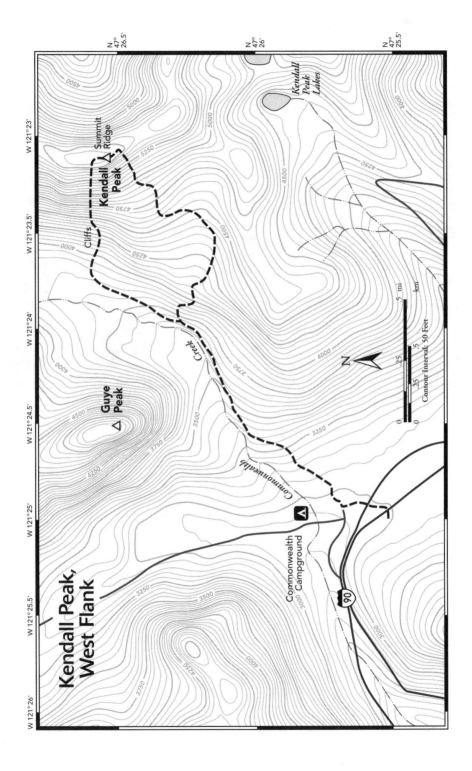

# Kendall Peak, West Flank

Guye Peak

Kendall Peak

Summit Ridge

Cliffs

Kendall Peak Lakes

Creek

Commonwealth

Commonwealth Campground

90

N

Contour Interval: 50 Feet

.5 mi

.5 km

.25

.25

W 121° 26'
W 121° 25.5'
W 121° 25'
W 121° 24.5'
W 121° 24'
W 121° 23.5'
W 121° 23'

N 47° 26.5'
N 47° 26'
N 47° 25.5'

**Kendall Peak, West Flank**

Cliffs

Kendall Peak from north–northwest. PHOTO BY MARTIN VOLKEN

Depending on the depth of the snowpack, a crossing can be quite awkward here.

At this point stay on the east side of the creek to 3,600 feet. Start climbing east here. If you encounter steep and cliff-studded terrain at around 4,100 feet instead of a gentle basin opening up, you might have turned east too early. At about 4,200 feet you'll enter an avalanche path on flat, heavily timbered terrain that might remind you of a human-made ski slope. This avalanche path is not indicated on the USGS map yet (about 2 hours to here). Follow this path until you reach more open terrain at about 4,600 feet. This open slope steepens and will guide you into the summit couloir, which is located a bit farther north. The couloir entrance often features avalanche debris; judge it carefully before entering. Favorable conditions, ski crampons, and good terrain management should send you to the summit col without taking off your skis.

Expect the following short summit ridge to have east-facing cornices. The west-facing slabs are layered unfavorably. Staying on the ridge crest is your best bet in the midwinter months. The climbing is easy if somewhat exposed, and the danger of stepping through a cornice cannot be overemphasized. It certainly wouldn't hurt to use a few pieces of protection on this short summit ridge.

From the summit (5,784 feet) start skiing with a short northerly traverse to a gentle dip in the west flank. Then ski the steep west flank (40 degrees in spots) down to the Commonwealth basin. Be aware that this slope unloads big avalanches. Assess slope stability before skiing this sporty route.

At around 4,300 feet you'll encounter some cliffs that can be easily negotiated on skier's left (south). Once you're in the basin, turn south and scoot back out to Alpental Road by staying east of Commonwealth Creek and eventually regaining your ascent track.

If you don't want to deal with the summit ridge and west flank descent, you can of course descend from the summit col via your ascent route.

The author on the summit ridge of Kendall Peak.
PHOTO BY PETER AVOLIO

# Red Mountain

**Tour distance:** About 8 km (5 miles)

**Tour time:** 4.5 to 5.5 hours

**Vertical gain/loss:** 2,910 feet/2,910 feet

**Difficulty rating:** Grade III

**Best season:** February through May

**Starting elevation/high point:** 2,980 feet/5,890 feet

**Gear required:** Standard ski-touring equipment

**Required fitness and skiing ability:** Good fitness and advanced skiing ability

**Map needed:** Snoqualmie Pass

I've met many people who wanted to ski the west face of Red Mountain. It's no surprise. This beautiful little pyramid looks very inviting when viewed from the upper Alpental Ski Area, and it offers one of the most consistent steeper slopes in the area.

**Approach:** Reach Snoqualmie Pass via Interstate 90 and take the west exit. Leave your car at the parking lot of the Summit West Ski Area.

Follow the parking lot access road until it turns east—just a short distance. Turn left off the road and start touring up to the Commonwealth Valley. Stay generally east of the creek until you reach a flat area next to Commonwealth Creek at around 3,560 feet. This is a key spot for many of the tours described. Up until the fall of 1999, there was a log crossing possibility at the flat spot.

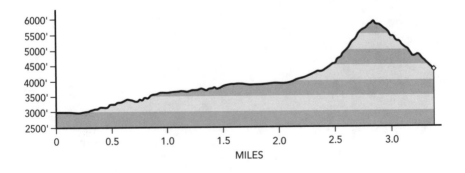

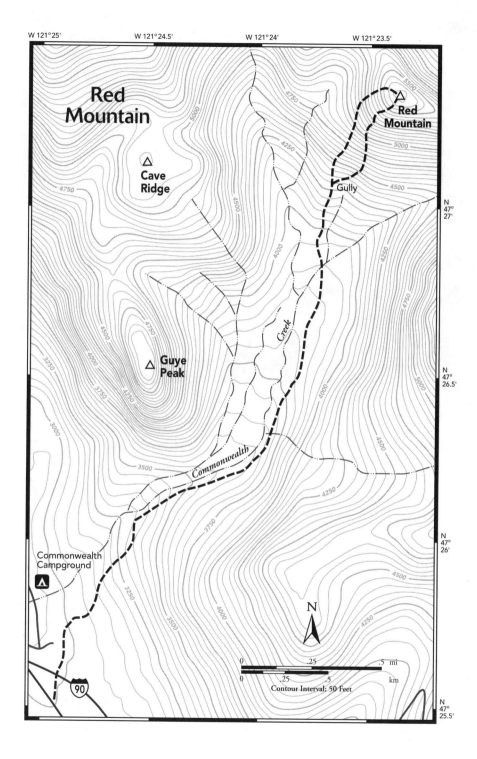

Red
Mountain

△ Cave
Ridge

Red
Mountain △

Gully

Creek

△ Guye
Peak

Commonwealth

Commonwealth
Campground

N

W 121° 25'    W 121° 24.5'    W 121° 24'    W 121° 23.5'

N 47° 27'
N 47° 26.5'
N 47° 26'
N 47° 25.5'

0        .25        .5  mi
0        .25        .5  km

Contour Interval: 50 Feet

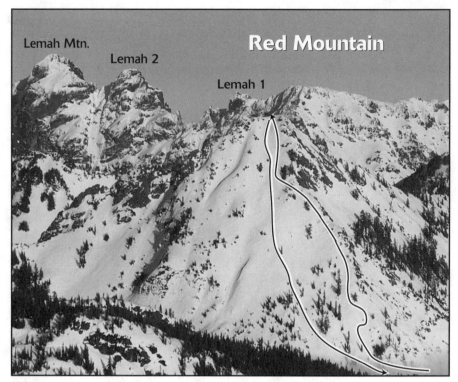

Red Mountain's west face. PHOTO BY MARTIN VOLKEN

Depending on the depth of the snowpack, a crossing can be quite awkward here.

Cross to the west side of the creek, but stay in the Commonwealth Valley. Proceed up the valley to about 4,000 feet (about 1.5 hours to here). Cross the creek back to the east side here and start skinning up the lower flanks of Red Mountain in a north-northeasterly direction. This will lead you into a gully that steepens and narrows at around 4,400 feet. Leave the gully here by traversing southeast for a few yards. This will set you in position for the upper flanks of Red Mountain's west face (4,500 feet; 2.5 hours to here).

A careful assessment of the slope is necessary. This slope has buried several people before. You're standing on the southern end of the west slope and can gain the south ridge easily from here if you don't feel good about the snow conditions on the slope. This may enable you to enjoy the scenic summit even if you don't ski the slope. Leave your skis here and climb the south ridge on foot to the summit. Return to your skis via the same route.

If you decide to tour up the slope, stick to its southern edge. Efficient track management will send you from the 4,500-foot level to the summit (5,890 feet) in about 1 hour (3.5 hours total to here).

The descent is straightforward. You can ski the center of the face to the 4,700-foot level. This steeper section is best navigated on skier's left, closer to the ascent track. From here ski out following your ascent track (4.5 to 5.5 hours to here).

# Lundin Peak

**Tour distance:** 9 km (5.6 miles)

**Tour time:** 6 to 7 hours

**Vertical gain/loss:** 3,207 feet/3,207 feet
(with satellite summit variation)

**Difficulty rating:** Grade III+

**Best season:** January through May

**Starting elevation/high point:** 2,980 feet/6,057 feet

**Gear required:** Standard ski-mountaineering equipment

**Required fitness and skiing ability:** Very good fitness and advanced skiing ability. Mountaineering experience is recommended for the summit section.

**Map needed:** Snoqualmie Pass

Lundin Peak is a rewarding introduction to ski mountaineering. The summit ridge makes the transition to basic but exposed climbing. The peak has a lofty feel, with unbeatable views into the rugged Lemah Range and the Middle Fork valley 4,000 feet below.

**Approach:** Reach Snoqualmie Pass via Interstate 90 and leave your car in the parking lot of the Summit West Ski Area.
    Follow the parking lot access road until it turns east—just a short distance. Turn left off the road and start touring up to the Commonwealth valley. Stay generally east of the creek until you reach a flat area next to Commonwealth Creek at around 3,560 feet. This is a key spot for many of the tours described.

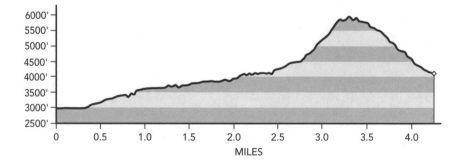

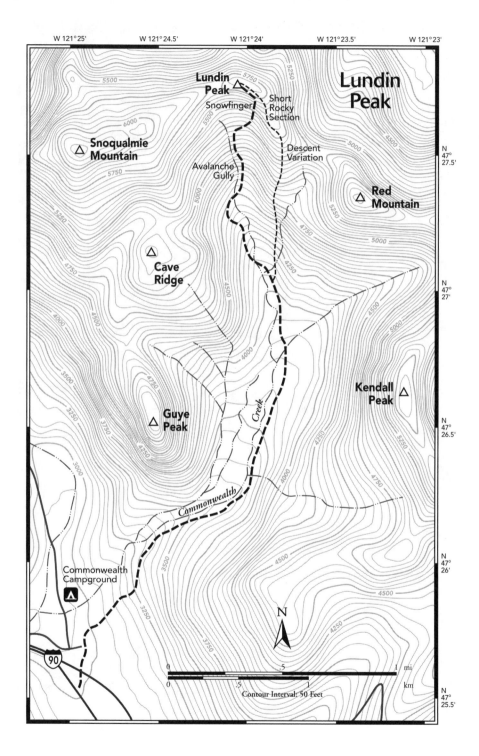

W 121°25'    W 121°24.5'    W 121°24'    W 121°23.5'    W 121°23'

Lundin
Peak

Snowfinger

Short
Rocky
Section

Descent
Variation

Snoqualmie
Mountain

Red
Mountain

Avalanche
Gully

Cave
Ridge

Guye
Peak

Kendall
Peak

Creek

Commonwealth

Commonwealth
Campground

90

N

0                    .5                    1 mi

0                    .5                    1
km

Contour Interval: 50 Feet

N 47° 27.5'

N 47° 27'

N 47° 26.5'

N 47° 26'

N 47° 25.5'

Lundin Peak

Ski
Depot

Lundin Peak's tricky summit block from the east. PHOTO BY MARTIN VOLKEN

Up until the fall of 1999, there was a log crossing possibility at the flat spot. Depending on the depth of the snowpack, a crossing can be quite awkward here.

Stay on the east side of the creek instead of crossing over to the Guye Peak side. You can tour up the Commonwealth basin quite easily by staying near Commonwealth Creek. Be aware of the avalanche slopes on your right coming down from the Kendall Peak area. At around 3,840 feet you'll have to cross a tributary stream that comes down from the Kendall Catwalk area. The crossing rarely presents a problem due to the size of the snowpack here.

Make sure not to get pulled up into this drainage in poor visibility. After the crossing keep touring north to the end of the basin at around 4,500 feet (2 hours to here).

You'll be due south of the short but steep south face of Lundin Peak. On the far-right or eastern border of the basin, you'll see an obvious gully. You can tour this all the way to the base of the even more prominent snow finger, which leads to the summit col.

It's crucial to assess stability at the 4,500-foot level before touring up the gully. It's also important to stay ahead of the sun for the ascent and (hopefully) the descent. Most of the slides that occur here are triggered by snow and ice falling into the snow finger or gully from the steep rock face that borders the ascent route to the east.

Good terrain management, a few kick turns, and some simple snow climbing will see you to the col at 5,860 feet (3.5 hours to here).

Deposit your skis and climb up the short snow flank to the west. The area below the summit is slabby and demands attention. Use appropriate gear (6,057 feet; about 4 hours to the summit).

For the descent I advise at least one rappel shortly below the summit. There are tree-anchor possibilities. From the summit col enjoy the ski down the snow finger and return to Snoqualmie Pass via your ascent track (6 to 7 hours).

**Variation:** An interesting variation on the return from the summit can be done by climbing up the short rocky section to the east of the col. This will put you on a little satellite peak of Lundin (5,920 feet). Follow a short but corniced snow ridge until you come to a rib that lets you ski down into the Commonwealth basin via the lower slopes of Red Mountain. This is also a great escape route if you feel that conditions in the gully have become too hazardous for a ski descent. And you'll get an excellent vantage point of the Red Mountain descent from here.

# Snoqualmie Mountain via Cave Ridge
## (Phantom Descent)

**Tour distance:** 7 km (4.3 miles)

**Tour time:** 6 hours

**Vertical gain/loss:** 3,298 feet/3,158 feet

**Difficulty rating:** Grade III

**Best season:** January through May

**Starting elevation/high point:** 2,980 feet/6,278 feet

**Gear required:** Standard ski-touring equipment

**Required fitness and skiing ability:** Good physical fitness and advanced skiing ability

**Map needed:** Snoqualmie Pass

This tour is a classic. The majority of it is visible from the freeway and the Alpental Ski Area. The summit views are outstanding, and the ski descent has one of the most direct lines in the area. The waterfall variation on the descent is one of the sportiest finishes of all the routes described in this book.

**Approach:** Reach Snoqualmie Pass via Interstate 90 and take the west exit. Leave your vehicle in the Summit West Ski Area parking lot. Carry your skis on Alpental Road to the summer turnoff for the Commonwealth basin parking lot.

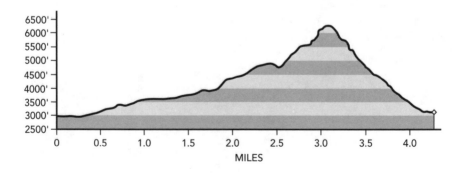

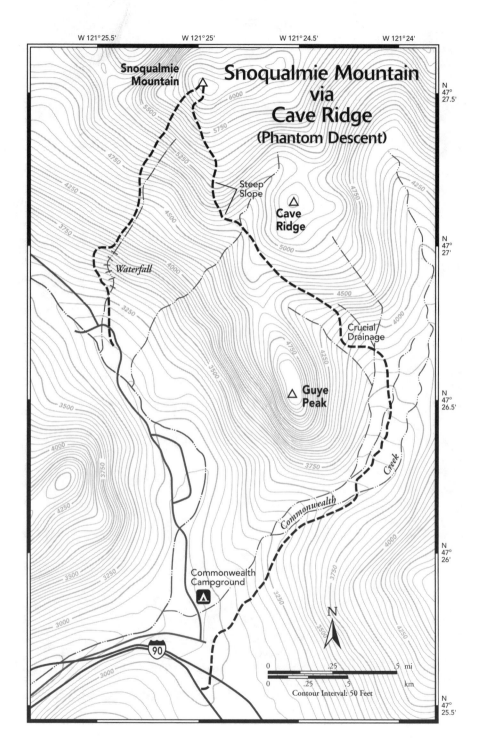

Snoqualmie Mountain via Cave Ridge (Phantom Descent)

Slot Couloir
Entrance

East
Summit

Waterfall
Direct Variation

**Snoqualmie Mountain**

Snoqualmie Mountain from southwest. PHOTO BY GINA VOLKEN

Follow the parking lot access road until it turns east—just a short distance. Turn left off the road and start touring up to the Commonwealth valley. Stay generally east of the creek until you reach a flat area next to Commonwealth Creek at around 3,560 feet. This is a key spot for many of the tours described. Up until the fall of 1999, there was a log crossing possibility at the flat spot. Depending on the depth of the snowpack, a crossing can be quite awkward here.

Cross to the west side of the creek here. Head for the northwest side of the valley and tour under the east flanks of Guye Peak until you reach the entrance of the distinct drainage (3,800 feet) that separates Guye Peak from Cave Ridge (about 1.5 hours to here).

This spot is crucial. Don't speculate here—anything but the drainage ascent will lead you into hazardous terrain. Go up this drainage to a prominent flat spot at 4,800 feet. Keep touring in a northwesterly direction, going around the south end of Cave Ridge to reach the toe of the south ridge of Snoqualmie Mountain (4,800 feet; 2.5 hours to here).

The bulge that lets you get onto the ridge is fairly steep and demands attention to snow stability. From here tour up in the vicinity of the ridge. At around 5,800 feet make a rising northwesterly traverse across the south slope to another gentle rib. Again, watch for stability. Stay on this slightly treed rib to the summit (6,278 feet; 4 hours to here).

The descent is straightforward. You should ski from the summit in a south-southwesterly direction. This will guide you very quickly into a very prominent avalanche path (not indicated on the map). The locals call this slide path the Phantom. This devastating slide occurred in February 1990 after a record 300-inch snowfall period in 20 days, which was followed by 3 inches of rain in 48 hours.

The descent leads over beautiful rollers, which certainly harbor dangers in the stress zones.

At around 3,800 feet you should arrive at the top of a waterfall. This waterfall has been skied, but it's steep (about 50 degrees) and requires the utmost care due to its slabby nature. Unless you're absolutely certain of the positive outcome of this sporty finish, it's advisable to navigate the falls to the west in the forest. Even here there are a few steep drops that require caution. Once you're below the falls, regain the slide path and ski down to Alpental Road by the maintenance buildings.

# Snoqualmie Mountain, East Summit

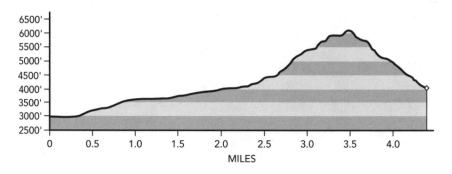

**Tour distance:** About 10 km (6.2 miles)

**Tour time:** 6 hours

**Vertical gain/loss:** 3,180 feet/3,180 feet

**Difficulty rating:** Grade II to III

**Best season:** January through May

**Starting elevation/high point:** 2,980 feet/6,180 feet

**Gear required:** Standard ski-touring equipment

**Required fitness and skiing ability:** Good physical fitness and advanced skiing ability

**Map needed:** Snoqualmie Pass

The Snoqualmie East Summit Tour is a fairly simple outing that will let you scope out many other touring objectives in the Commonwealth valley. It also offers great skiing and great views into the Lemah Range and the lonely Middle Fork valley.

**Approach:** From Interstate 90 take the Snoqualmie Pass west exit and leave your car at the Summit West Ski Area parking lot.

Follow the parking lot access road until it turns east—just a short distance. Turn left off the road and start touring up to the Commonwealth valley. Stay generally east of the creek until you reach a flat area next to Commonwealth Creek

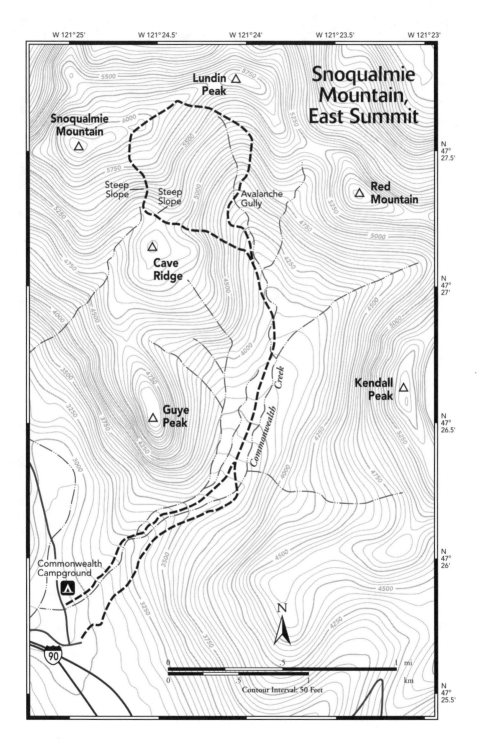

## Snoqualmie Mountain, East Summit

W 121° 25'  W 121° 24.5'  W 121° 24'  W 121° 23.5'  W 121° 23'

Lundin Peak

Snoqualmie Mountain

Red Mountain

Steep Slope

Steep Slope

Avalanche Gully

Cave Ridge

Kendall Peak

Guye Peak

Commonwealth Creek

Commonwealth Campground

90

N 47° 27.5'

N 47° 27'

N 47° 26.5'

N 47° 26'

N 47° 25.5'

N

0        .5        1 mi
0     .5        1 km

Contour Interval: 50 Feet

Snoqualmie Mountain from the southwest. PHOTO BY MARTIN VOLKEN

at around 3,560 feet. This is a key spot for many of the tours described. Up until the fall of 1999, there was a log crossing possibility at the flat spot. Depending on the depth of the snowpack, a crossing can be quite awkward here.

Cross to the west side of the creek, then continue up the Commonwealth basin. Make sure not to get dragged over too far to the west once you're past Guye Peak; there's a little drainage that would lead you into steeper terrain than necessary. Exit the forest at 4,200 feet (about 2 hours to here).

Continue touring for a short distance into an upper basin below the valley headwall at 4,500 feet. You'll see a gully on the right side of the valley headwall that leads out of the basin (the same gully used in Tour 9, Lundin Peak). It's important to assess the stability of this gully and the objective dangers in the snow-loaded cliffs on its east side. The gully is essentially an avalanche path: Remember that before committing to the following ascent. The gully narrows and then opens back up. You'll see a stand of bigger trees on the top left of the gully (5,200 feet; 2.5 to 3 hours to here). If you were to continue straight up, you'd end up in the snow finger that leads up to the summit col of Lundin Peak.

Go past these trees and then start ascending in a northwesterly traverse with the south face of Lundin looming above. You'll eventually gain the gentle ridge between Lundin Peak and Snoqualmie Mountain at around 6,000 feet. From here keep traversing along the ridge until you gain the knob of Snoqualmie's east summit at 6,180 feet (4 hours to here).

Enjoy the views. This summit can serve as a starting point for several ski descents, such as the Middle Fork descent and the Crooked Couloir. Keep your options open.

The descent for this tour takes you down the beautiful south slope toward the headwaters of a little unnamed creek north of Cave Ridge (5,100 feet). The skiing here is beautiful, but the descent steepens substantially at the 5,500-foot level; stability needs to be assessed. You can always return via your ascent route or use the somewhat gentler rib that runs in a south-southeasterly direction off Snoqualmie Mountain's east summit. This will lead you into the same area just north of Cave Ridge. From here ski southeast down the steep but short drainage into the Commonwealth basin at 4,200 feet. This drainage is located north of Cave Ridge. Note that the entrance into the drainage nears 40 degrees.

From the 4,200-foot level in the Commonwealth basin, scoot out along the west side of Commonwealth Creek past the east face of Guye Peak out to Alpental Road. Please avoid the private property of Sahale Lodge near the road. It can easily be bypassed to the east (6 hours to here).

If the drainage seems too steep or unstable, follow the little unnamed creek that runs south on the west side of Cave Ridge until you can turn left. Ascend the gentle bench just south of Cave Ridge, and from there ski down the prominent drainage between Guye Peak and Cave Ridge into the Commonwealth basin (3,800 feet).

Now you can follow the west side of Commonwealth Creek out to Alpental Road—again, avoiding the Sahale Ski Club private property (6 hours to here).

# The Slot Couloir

**Tour distance:** 8 km (5 miles)

**Tour time:** 5 to 7 hours

**Vertical gain/loss:** 4,038 feet/4,038 feet

**Difficulty rating:** Grade IV, due to the difficult ski descent

**Best season:** March through May

**Starting elevation/high point:** 3,120 feet/6,278 feet

**Gear required:** Standard ski mountaineering equipment

**Required fitness and skiing ability:** Very good physical fitness and expert skiing ability

**Map needed:** Snoqualmie Pass

The Slot Couloir is one of the best tours in this selection. It contains many of the elements of a challenging ski tour and will let you make the transition to steep-ski alpinism. The descent is committing; in the remote atmosphere of the couloir, your judgment call will become an experience in itself. The Slot Couloir was first done by Alpental Pro Patroller Jan Kordel.

**Approach:** Take Interstate 90 to the Snoqualmie Pass west exit. Turn left at the stop sign and drive on Alpental Road to the main parking lot of the Alpental Ski Area.

From the Snow Lake Trailhead on the north side of the main parking lot, start touring through big timber. You're essentially following the river upstream for about 1 kilometer (0.6 mile). You'll cross the Phantom slide path at 3,100

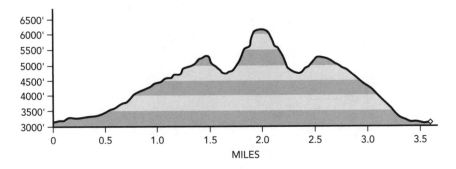

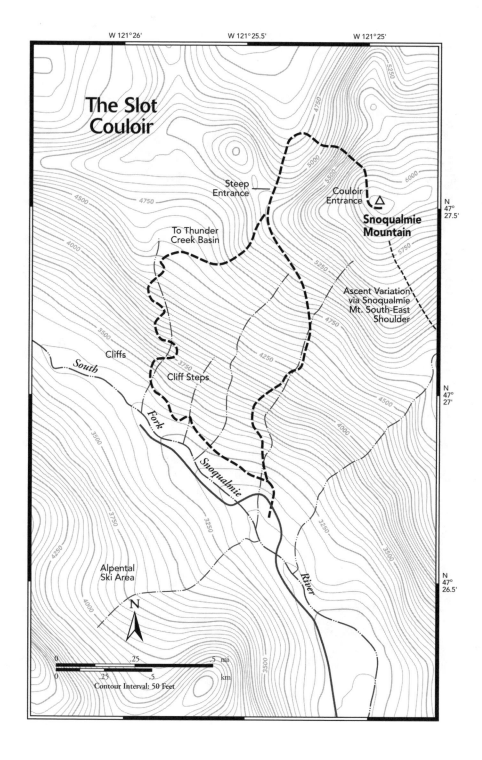

The Slot
Couloir

Steep
Entrance

Couloir
Entrance

Snoqualmie
Mountain

To Thunder
Creek Basin

Ascent Variation
via Snoqualmie
Mt. South-East
Shoulder

Cliffs

South

Cliff Steps

Fork

Snoqualmie

River

Alpental
Ski Area

N

W 121° 26'    W 121° 25.5'    W 121° 25'

N 47° 27.5'

N 47° 27'

N 47° 26.5'

0        .25        .5 mi
0     .25     .5 km
Contour Interval: 50 Feet

Snoqualmie Mountain's Slot Couloir. PHOTO BY SCOTT SCHELL

feet. At around 3,400 feet start climbing up to the north along a gentle and not very pronounced ridge. If you go too far, you'll find yourself in cliffy terrain.

At about 4,400 feet (1 to 1.5 hours to here) the terrain angles back substantially. The terrain above you is open to the left and bowl-like on the right. It's important to reach the southern extension of this "half bowl" at 4,690 feet. From here get out of the bowl and tour up in a northeasterly direction to the distinct notch at the base of Snoqualmie Mountain's west ridge (5,240 feet; 2 to 2.5 hours to here). This spot is crucial.

From the notch ski down the steep but short gully that lets you enter the uppermost reaches of Thunder Creek on the northwest side of Snoqualmie Mountain. (This short descent will give you a first indication of the snow conditions for the Slot Couloir descent.)

At 4,800 feet turn right; you'll see the steep and uniform Slot Couloir. (If you've gone too far, you'll see the exit of the Crooked Couloir.) From here pack your skis and start climbing up the couloir.

You have to feel good about the stability, since there are no escape routes once you're in the couloir. You might encounter a shrund at the bottom. Continue to the top of the couloir, constantly checking the snow stability. At the top you'll find yourself a very short distance west of Snoqualmie Mountain's summit (6,278 feet; 4 to 5 hours to here).

The descent is fun, but committing. It might be worthwhile to build a snow anchor at the top of the couloir and ski belayed for a rope length to make your final assessment of the slope. The average steepness ranges around 40 degrees.

Once you're out of the couloir, turn south and tour back up to the west notch of Snoqualmie Mountain (5,240 feet; 5 to 6 hours to here).

From here enjoy the Phantom descent down to the parking lot. This descent leads over beautiful rollers, which certainly harbor dangers in the stress zones.

At around 3,800 feet you'll arrive at the top of a waterfall. This waterfall has been skied, but it's steep (about 50 degrees) and requires the utmost care due to its slabby nature. Unless you're absolutely certain of the positive outcome of this sporty finish, it's advisable to navigate the falls to the west in the forest. Even here there are a few steep drops that require caution. Once you're below the falls, regain the slide path and ski down to Alpental Road by the maintenance buildings (6 to 7 hours to here).

If conditions are straightforward, the descent can certainly be approached via Cave Ridge and Snoqualmie Mountain's southeast shoulder. For a route description, see Tour 10.

# The Crooked Couloir

**Tour distance:** 8 km (5 miles)

**Tour time:** 5 to 7 hours

**Vertical gain/loss:** 3,880 feet/3,740 feet

**Difficulty rating:** Grade III+

**Best season:** January through May

**Starting elevation/high point:** 2,980 feet/6,180 feet

**Gear required:** Standard ski-touring gear, plus harness and rappel device, and one 120-foot rope

**Required fitness and skiing ability:** Very good fitness and expert skiing ability

**Map needed:** Snoqualmie Pass

The Crooked Couloir Tour sheds new light on Snoqualmie Mountain. It takes you to the surprisingly rugged and remote-feeling west side of the peak and rewards you with a spectacular ski descent.

**Approach:** Take Interstate 90 to the Snoqualmie Pass west exit. Leave your vehicle at the Summit West parking lot.

Start your tour by walking under the I–90 overpass on Alpental Road. After about 600 feet leave the road by the Commonwealth access road and turn north up into the Commonwealth valley. Stay east of Commonwealth Creek until you come to the flat area at about 3,560 feet.

Cross the creek here and proceed north on the west side of the creek until you find the distinct drainage between Cave Ridge and Guye Peak. Follow this

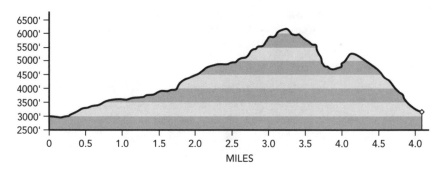

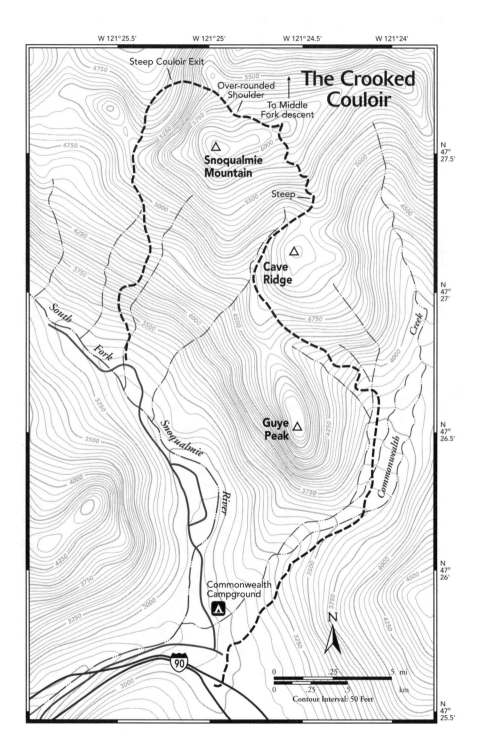

The Crooked Couloir

Steep Couloir Exit
Over-rounded Shoulder
To Middle Fork descent

Snoqualmie Mountain

Steep

Cave Ridge

Guye Peak

South Fork

Snoqualmie River

Commonwealth Creek

Commonwealth Campground

90

N

0        .25        .5 mi
0     .25      .5    km

Contour Interval: 50 Feet

W 121° 25.5'
W 121° 25'
W 121° 24.5'
W 121° 24'

N 47° 27.5'
N 47° 27'
N 47° 26.5'
N 47° 26'
N 47° 25.5'

Northwest side of Snoqualmie Mountain. PHOTO BY SCOTT SCHELL

drainage to the top at 4,800 feet. (This is the same start you'd take on Tour 10, Cave Ridge.) From here tour around the southern toe of Cave Ridge, lose about 100 feet of elevation, and continue in a northwesterly direction until you reach the pretty drainage that divides Cave Ridge from the southeast flanks of Snoqualmie Mountain (2 hours to here). This is where you branch away from the Cave Ridge Tour route. Continue up the drainage in a northeasterly direction to about 5,100 feet.

Gain the rounded southeast ridge of Snoqualmie Mountain's east summit. Follow this ridge, or the southeast flanks (depending on snow stability), to the east summit (6,180 feet; 3.5 hours to here). The lower slopes and the entrance to the ridge are both steep and demand attention to snow stability.

From the summit descend northwest across a rib into a gentle bowl. This is the top of the Crooked Couloir. You should see the couloir getting steeper and narrower, and disappearing to the west. (If you don't, you might still be too far east. This is the entrance to the north side descent.) The couloir starts out bowl-like, then narrows and seems to dead-end into a rock face to the north. Here it steepens and makes an elegant turn to the west. The couloir exit is quite steep (45 degrees) and may have ice bulges. You should be able to pass this problem on the north side, or you may have to rappel over the bulges. There are tree anchors. From here ski the remaining turns into the Thunder Creek basin.

From the basin turn south and tour and climb up to the distinct notch at the bottom of Snoqualmie Mountain's west ridge at 5,240 feet. The last portion of this climb is steep and could present a sizable hazard (5 hours to here). Then ski the Phantom avalanche path to the Alpental Ski Area (6 hours to here).

If the west ridge notch seems too dangerous, proceed to the gentle saddle at 4,860 feet on the west side of the Thunder Creek basin. From this saddle you can proceed south to Point 4,958, then ski in a southeasterly direction to the ski area (6 to 7 hours to here).

# Snoqualmie Middle Fork Descent

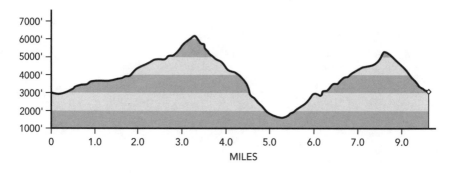

**Tour distance:** 15 km (9.3 miles)

**Tour time:** 8 to 9 hours

**Vertical gain/loss:** 6,820 feet/6,680 feet

**Difficulty rating:** Grade III+ to IV

**Best season:** January through March

**Starting elevation/high point:** 2,980 feet/6,180 feet (Middle Fork is at 1,600 feet)

**Gear required:** Standard ski-touring equipment

**Required fitness and skiing ability:** Excellent fitness and advanced skiing ability

**Map needed:** Snoqualmie Pass

A 4,500-foot vertical descent is a beautiful thing—especially off a 6,180-foot mountain. Apart from great skiing, this tour will be a good endurance test without having to resort to the "jo-jo" method. An adequate low-elevation snow level is obviously crucial for this tour.

**Approach:** Take Interstate 90 to the Snoqualmie Pass west exit. Leave your vehicle at the Summit West parking lot.

Follow the parking lot access road until it turns east—just a short distance. Turn left off the road and start touring up to the Commonwealth valley. Stay generally east of the creek until you reach a flat area next to Commonwealth Creek

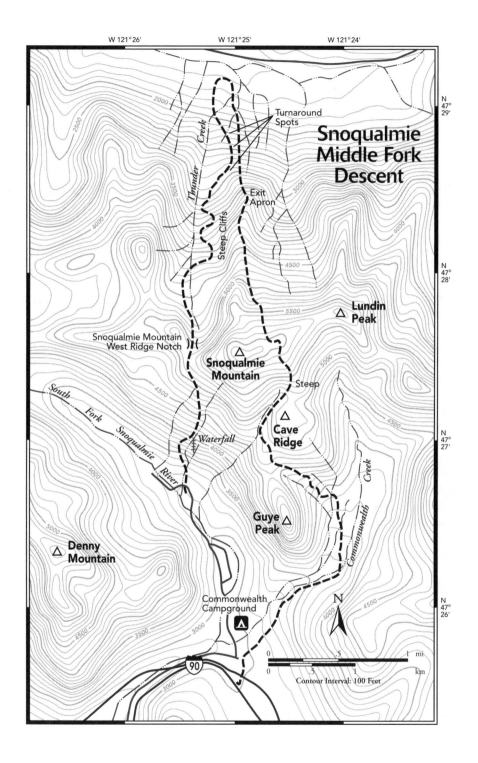

Snoqualmie
Middle Fork
Descent

Turnaround
Spots

Exit
Apron

Thunder Creek

Steep Cliffs

△ Lundin
Peak

Snoqualmie Mountain
West Ridge Notch

△
Snoqualmie
Mountain

Steep

South Fork Snoqualmie River

Waterfall

△
Cave
Ridge

Guye △
Peak

Commonwealth Creek

Denny △
Mountain

Commonwealth
Campground

[A]

90

N

0　　　　　.5　　　　1 mi
0　　　.5　　1　　km
Contour Interval: 100 Feet

at around 3,560 feet. This is a key spot for many of the tours described. Up until the fall of 1999, there was a log crossing possibility at the flat spot. Depending on the depth of the snowpack, a crossing can be quite awkward here.

Cross to the west side of the creek here. Head for the northwest side of the valley and tour under the east flanks of Guye Peak until you reach the entrance of the distinct drainage (3,800 feet) that separates Guye Peak from Cave Ridge (about 1.5 hours to here).

This spot is crucial. Don't speculate here—anything but the drainage ascent will lead you into hazardous terrain. Go up this drainage to a prominent flat spot at 4,800 feet. Cross this flat spot in a northwesterly direction, then drop about 100 feet to reach a little drainage located immediately west of Cave Ridge.

Turn northeast here and follow the drainage up to about 5,100 feet. Then turn northwest and skin up the steep slopes to Snoqualmie Mountain's east summit. You can gain the southeast ridge and get to the summit from there (6,180 feet; 4 hours to here). But be careful: You'll have to assess the stability of these slopes due to steepness and exposure.

To descend, ski right off the east summit (or slightly west of it) in a northerly direction. There's a narrow trough bordered by the eastern ridge of the Thunder Creek basin on skier's left. The skiing is beautiful, and the trough will eventually bring you right onto the eastern ridge—quite unusual but ever so much fun (4,600 feet). From here you'll ski right on the ridge (very steep on skier's left!). At 4,100 feet the ridge gives way to a broadening slope that's quite steep. Keep to the left edge of this slope and reach gentle terrain at 3,000 feet. From here ski down as far as the snowpack allows (1,600 feet; 5 hours to here).

You'll have to regain Snoqualmie Mountain's west notch from here. To do so, start touring back up your ascent tracks to about 2,500 feet, then tour west until you're in the lower basin of the Thunder Creek drainage. The terrain steepens between 3,000 and 3,400 feet but is certainly tourable. In the upper basin the touring is simple and scenic. The impressive west face of Snoqualmie Mountain will be on your left. Keep touring to about 4,600 feet, where the terrain steepens.

Continue in a southerly direction toward the distinct west ridge notch of Snoqualmie Mountain at 5,240 feet (about 8 hours to here). The last part of this ascent is steep and may present a sizable hazard.

From the west ridge notch, ski in a southeasterly direction to the Phantom avalanche path; ski down this path to the maintenance buildings of the Alpental Ski Area. Avoid the waterfall at about 3,800 feet by skirting it to the west in the forest (9 hours to here).

If you don't feel good about the final slope, keep touring in a westerly direction from the 4,600-foot level to a gentle saddle at 4,860 feet on the west side of the Thunder Creek basin. Proceed south to Point 4,958, then ski in a southeasterly direction to the ski area maintenance buildings.

# Pineapple Basin

**Tour distance:** About 6 km (3.7 miles)

**Tour time:** 3 to 4 hours

**Vertical gain/loss:** 1,720 feet/1,720 feet

**Difficulty rating:** Grade I to II

**Best season:** December through May

**Starting elevation/high point:** 3,220 feet/4,940 feet

**Gear required:** Standard ski-touring gear

**Required fitness and skiing ability:** Good physical fitness and intermediate to advanced skiing ability

**Map needed:** Snoqualmie Pass

This tour is an excellent introduction to the Alpental backcountry. It takes you to the pretty Pineapple basin and past the east face of the Tooth, which is many a Seattle mountaineer's first summit. Even though the tour is short and in the immediate vicinity of the Alpental Ski Area lift access, you must consider the avalanche potential of this area. It's worthwhile checking with the local ski patrol about current snow stability.

**Approach:** Take Interstate 90 to the Snoqualmie Pass west summit exit. Drive on Alpental Road to the uppermost parking lot (3,220 feet). Leave your vehicle here.

From the parking lot you'll see a groomed path leading deeper into the Alpental valley. Follow this path to its end. From here you continue up the val-

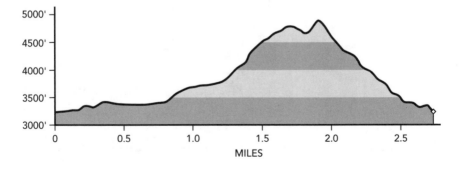

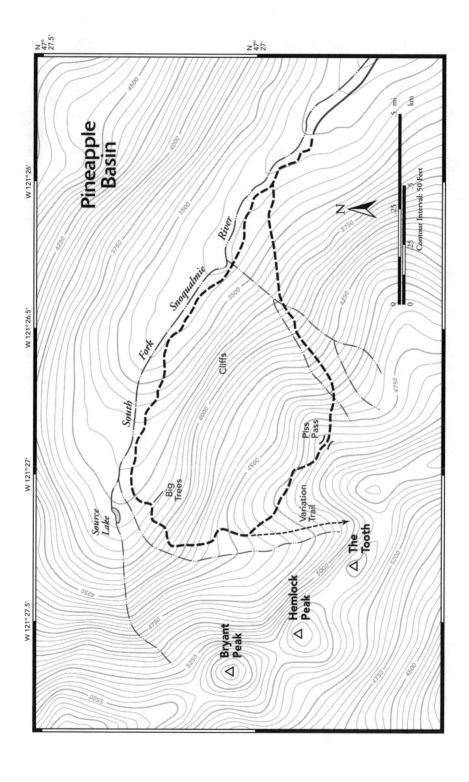

Pineapple Basin from the north. PHOTO BY MARTIN VOLKEN

ley, staying well above and south of the Snoqualmie River. Be aware that the north slopes of the valley are steep and very avalanche prone. Absolutely abandon this tour if snow stability is less than good. Just before you reach Source Lake at 3,760 feet, start touring up in a southerly direction to a little tributary valley that's bordered by the steep northeast faces of Bryant and Hemlock Peaks, and the Tooth on its west side.

Make sure to stay on the east side of the creek as you tour. This is certainly the objectively safest way to reach the gentle upper valley at 4,400 feet (2 hours to here). Then keep touring up the valley in a southerly direction until you reach the 4,700-foot level. Turn east-northeast and reach the vicinity of a small but very distinct pass known as Piss Pass (4,940 feet). This is your high point. Ski off Piss Pass on skier's right and enjoy one of Alpental's better backcountry runs down to the catch road at around 3,400 feet. You can ski straight down the drainage or trend slightly right. In either case be aware of the smaller cliff drop-offs—which are characteristic of the whole Denny Mountain north slope.

**Variation:** A very attractive option in this area is to ski to the obvious pass at the far southern end of the Pineapple basin. From here you can descend to your car via your ascent track from Source Lake, or regain the described route that leads to Piss Pass.

# Snow Lake Divide

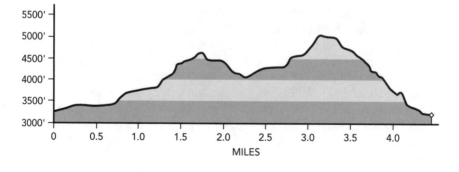

**Tour distance:** 7 km (4.3 miles)

**Tour time:** 3 to 5 hours

**Vertical gain/loss:** 2,250 feet/2,240 feet

**Difficulty rating:** Grade I to II

**Best season:** January through May

**Starting elevation/high point:** 3,220 feet/4,958 feet

**Gear required:** Standard ski-touring equipment

**Required fitness and skiing ability:** Good fitness and solid intermediate skiing ability

**Map needed:** Snoqualmie Pass

This excellent introductory tour takes you into some scenic portions of the immediate Alpental backcountry. This is one of the least committing tours in this book and comes into condition very quickly.

**Approach:** Take Interstate 90 to the Snoqualmie Pass west summit exit. Drive on Alpental Road to the uppermost parking lot (3,220 feet).

From the parking lot you'll see a groomed path leading deeper into the Alpental valley. Follow this path to its end. From here you continue up the valley, staying well above and south of the Snoqualmie River. Be aware that the north slopes of the valley are steep and very avalanche prone. Once you reach Source Lake at 3,760 feet (1 hour to here), tour up the open slope that comes down from the Chair Peak basin. At around 4,300 feet start trending north

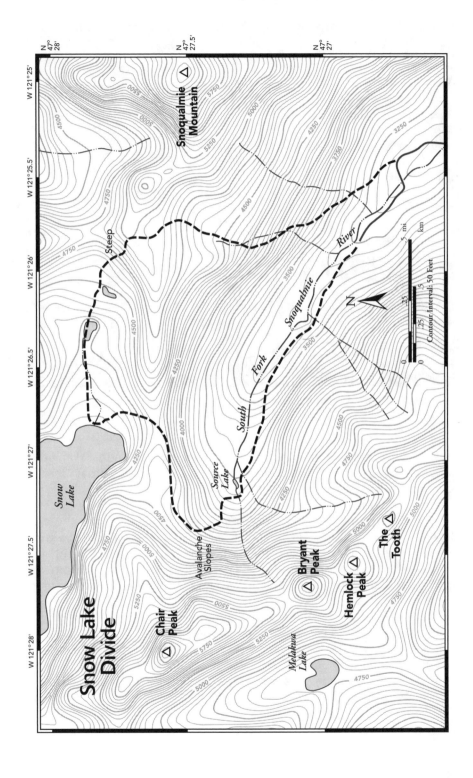

South Shoulder    Chair Peak    Kaleetan Peak    Mt. Roosevelt

Snow Lake

Chair Peak and Snow Lake area from east. PHOTO BY SCOTT SCHELL

toward a flat spot (4,450 feet). You're now on Snow Lake Divide. Ski along the divide in a northeasterly direction until you reach the obvious pass that lets you ski down to Snow Lake (4,016 feet; 2 hours to here).

From Snow Lake tour eastward for about 1.5 kilometers (0.9 miles). At 4,600 feet the terrain steepens abruptly. Turn south and ascend the steep slopes southward to the col at Point 4,958 (about 3 hours to here). (If you don't feel comfortable with the snow conditions on this short but north-facing slope, you can return to the Snow Lake Divide col via the descent route.) From Point 4,958 ski straight south along a gentle rib that borders much steeper terrain to the west.

Don't attempt to ski all the way to the river: A crossing to get directly to your vehicle may be quite difficult and dangerous. You'll be better off if you start skiing in a southeasterly direction once you hit the 3,400-foot level. This should bring you to Alpental Road near the ski area maintenance buildings. From there walk the short distance back up Alpental Road to your vehicle.

# Chair Peak, North Slope Descent

*Tour* 17

**Tour distance:** 8.5 km (5.3 miles)

**Tour time:** 5 hours

**Vertical gain/loss:** 3,140 feet/3,140 feet

**Difficulty rating:** Grade II to III

**Best season:** January through mid-April

**Starting elevation/high point:** 3,220 feet/5,900 feet

**Gear required:** Standard ski-touring gear

**Required fitness and skiing ability:** Very good fitness and advanced skiing ability

**Map needed:** Snoqualmie Pass

This is a moderate tour in a spectacular environment in the upper Alpental valley.

**Approach:** Take Interstate 90 to the Snoqualmie Pass west exit. Drive on Alpental Road to the uppermost parking lot (3,200 feet).

From the parking lot you'll see a groomed path leading deeper into the Alpental valley. Follow this path to its end. From here you continue up the valley, staying well above and south of the Snoqualmie River. Be aware that the north slopes of the valley are steep and very avalanche prone. Absolutely abandon this tour if snow stability is less than good. Once you reach Source Lake at 3,760 feet (1 hour to here), tour up the open slope that comes down

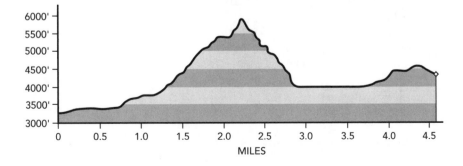

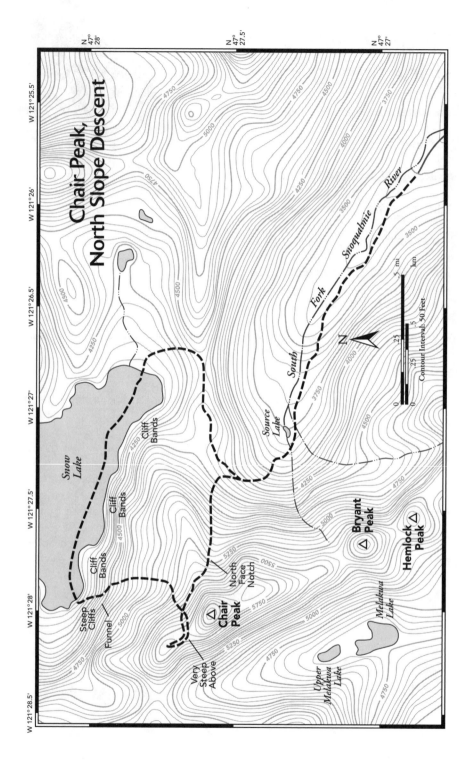

# Chair Peak,
# North Slope Descent

Contour Interval: 50 Feet

Snow Lake

Cliff Bands

Cliff Bands

Cliff Bands

Cliff Bands

Steep Cliffs

Funnel

Very Steep Above

Chair Peak

North Face Notch

Source Lake

South Fork Snoqualmie River

Bryant Peak

Hemlock Peak

Melakwa Lake

Upper Melakwa Lake

N 47° 28'

N 47° 27.5'

N 47° 27'

W 121° 28.5'

W 121° 28'

W 121° 27.5'

W 121° 27'

W 121° 26.5'

W 121° 26'

W 121° 25.5'

South Shoulder    Chair Peak    Kaleetan Peak    Mt. Roosevelt

**Chair Peak and Snow Lake Area**

Chair Peak and Snow Lake area from east. PHOTO BY SCOTT SCHELL

from the Chair Peak basin. At around 4,300 feet start trending north toward a flat spot (4,450 feet). From here you have to ascend the steep slopes (going west) up into the Chair Peak basin.

The northern rim of the basin shows a very distinct notch (5,360 feet), which leads from the basin onto the north slopes below Chair Peak's spectacular north face. Climb from the basin into the notch (a short section of about 45- to 50-degree snow climbing and 2.5 hours to here). Then traverse the north slope directly under Chair Peak's north face. Here's another point to stop and evaluate stability. You must feel good about the conditions before committing to this ski descent. Traverse the north slope until you reach the distinct saddle at the bottom of Chair Peak's northwest ridge (5,900 feet)—which is itself a short but interesting ridge climb to the summit (3 hours to here).

This tour's ski descent follows the western edge of the north slopes down to the western edge of Snow Lake. This will funnel you into a gully that's bordered by some steep cliffs on its west side. The gully opens back up, however, from there your descent to the lake is simple. If you end up too far east, you'll have to negotiate cliffs that make skiing down to the lake somewhat adventurous. Furthermore, skirting the south rim of the lake is tedious and dangerous if the lake proves uncrossable. For this reason I don't recommend this tour in early winter. Skirting the lake on the north side is doable, but time consuming and not very interesting.

From the western edge of the lake, ski across the lake in a southeasterly direction and skin back up to Snow Lake Divide at 4,450 feet (4.5 hours to here). Skiing straight down to the Alpental valley is possible but quite steep and cliff studded. It's better to skin west, gaining 100 feet of elevation, until you reach the flat spot mentioned as part of your ascent from Source Lake. Then ski down to Source Lake and out to the parking lot (about 5 hours to here).

# Chair Peak, South Shoulder

**Tour distance:** 7 km (4.3 miles)

**Tour time:** 5 to 6 hours

**Vertical gain/loss:** 2,780 feet/2,780 feet

**Difficulty rating:** Grade III

**Best season:** March through May

**Starting elevation/high point:** 3,220 feet/6,000 feet

**Gear required:** Standard ski-touring gear, plus harness, crampons, ice ax, rope, some slings, and a few locking carabiners

**Required fitness and skiing ability:** Very good physical fitness and expert skiing ability

**Map needed:** Snoqualmie Pass

The south shoulder of Chair Peak doesn't get many visitors—especially not in the winter months. Although it's short, this tour is rather demanding. Good track management is important if you're to make it to the high point in time. Much of the ascent and descent route cruises through avalanche terrain; good snow-stability assessment skills are crucial. The skiing is far from extreme, but it is committing and can be sporty. Proper tour planning is very important before you embark on this short but spectacular day trip.

**Approach:** Take Interstate 90 to the Snoqualmie Pass west exit. Drive on

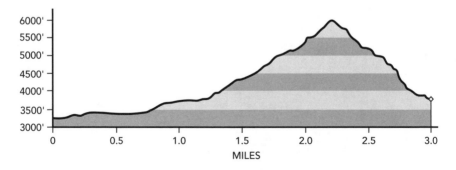

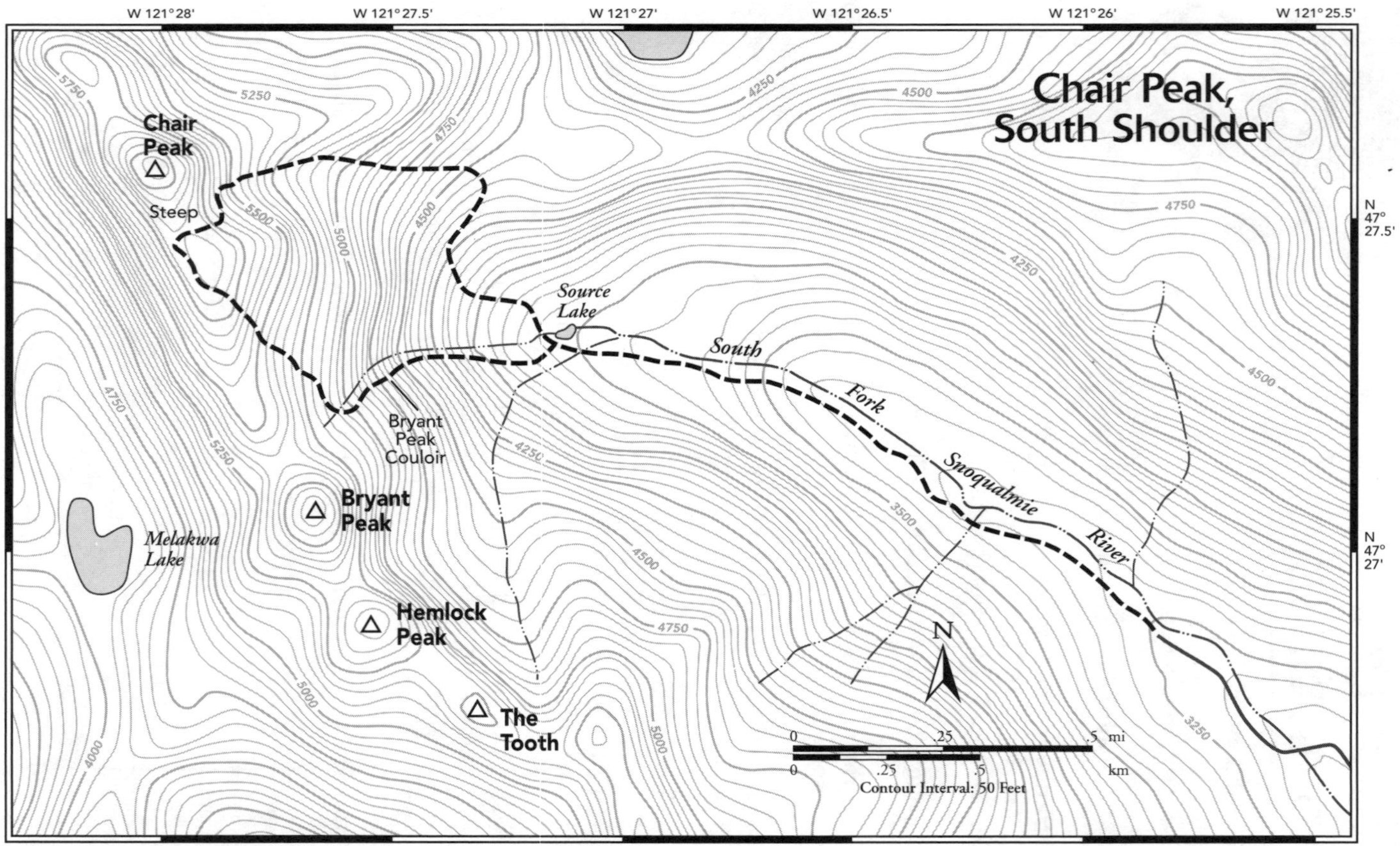

# Chair Peak, South Shoulder

N 47° 27.5'

N 47° 27'

W 121° 25.5'

W 121° 26'

W 121° 26.5'

W 121° 27'

W 121° 27.5'

W 121° 28'

Contour Interval: 50 Feet

.5 mi

km

.25

.5

.25

0

0

N

Snoqualmie River

South Fork

Source Lake

Bryant Peak Couloir

Bryant Peak

Hemlock Peak

The Tooth

Chair Peak

Steep

Melakwa Lake

3250

3500

4000

4250

4500

4750

5000

4250

4500

4750

5000

5250

4750

5250

5500

5750

4750

4500

4250

Chair Peak,
South Shoulder

Bryant Peak Col

To Source
Lake

Bryant Peak Col from the northeast. PHOTO BY SCOTT SCHELL

Alpental Road to the uppermost parking lot (3,220 feet). Start your tour here.

From the parking lot you'll see a groomed path leading deeper into the Alpental valley. Follow this path to its end. From here you continue up the valley, staying well above and south of the Snoqualmie River. Be aware that the north slopes of the valley are steep and very avalanche prone. Absolutely abandon this tour if snow stability is less than good. Once you reach Source Lake at 3,760 feet (1 hour to here), tour up the open slope that comes down from the Chair Peak basin. At around 4,300 feet start trending north toward a flat spot (4,450 feet). From here you have to ascend the steep slopes (going west) up into the Chair Peak basin (about 2 hours to here).

Keep touring farther up into the basin. You'll see a steep snow slope that extends to a little col on the basin's southwestern end. There's avalanche terrain all around you; solid stability evaluations need to be made before you commit to the climb up to the col. If conditions are favorable, you can tour up all the way to the col at 5,960 feet without taking off your skis. Otherwise you might have to put on crampons or simply boot-kick some steps up the final steep slope (about 3 hours to here).

Once you're on the col, turn southeast and follow the easy, scenic ridge for a short distance to the south shoulder. This ridge may be heavily corniced! After about 300 feet (100 meters) you'll reach a distinct spot on the south shoulder's summit col (6,000 feet): You want to start skiing here. If you find yourself on top of a cornice, you most likely didn't find the proper entrance. The col faces directly out the Alpental valley and usually doesn't build up cornices. (See topo on page 87.)

The skiing isn't difficult, but it is quite spectacular with Source Lake huddled more than 2,000 feet directly below you as you are make your turns. There are two distinct rollers on the upper 600 feet of the descent. Ski over the first one and pass the second one on the left. Trend slightly left from here, since it's very important to catch an exit ramp at around 5,100 feet. A big cliff—5,000 feet—runs from the north edge of the slope to the Bryant Peak Couloir, which is on the far southern end of the slope. The exit ramp on the north end and the Bryant Peak Couloir entrance on the south are your two ways around the cliff band.

This ramp will guide you north for about 600 feet (200 meters) until you can start making turns again down the southwestern edge of the slope that you ascended previously to get into the Chair Peak basin. From here ski down to Source Lake (about 4 hours to here). This is an avalanche chute; you can traverse north a little longer and reach gentler descent terrain.

If the Bryant Peak Couloir is of interest, you need to pass the second roller on the right and keep trending right. You should reach the southern edge of the cliff at just about 5,000 feet. It merges here with the Bryant Peak Couloir. The entrance into the couloir can be tricky, because it often shows small lateral glide cracks. This has to do with the rock-slabby nature of the couloir itself.

Once you're in the couloir, follow it to about 4,000 feet, where it splits. There's a smaller inviting couloir that keeps the fall line, and the bigger couloir that turns somewhat to the right. Take the bigger one: The smaller one ends with a little cliff drop that can be quite annoying, depending on the snowpack. From here ski down to Source Lake and then out the Alpental valley to the parking lot (5 to 6 hours to here).

**Scott Schell in the
upper Chair Peak basin.**
*Photo by Martin Volken*

# Chair Peak Circumnavigation

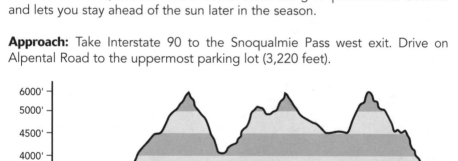

**Tour distance:** 12 km (7.4 miles)

**Tour time:** 6 to 9 hours

**Vertical gain/loss:** 4,510 feet/4,510 feet

**Difficulty rating:** Grade III-plus

**Best season:** January through May

**Starting elevation/high point:** 3,220 feet/5,460 feet

**Gear required:** Standard ski-touring equipment

**Required fitness and skiing ability:** Very good physical fitness and advanced skiing ability

**Map needed:** Snoqualmie Pass

This tour around the dominating peak of the Alpental valley has all the elements to become a classic: beautiful ski descents, somewhat committing terrain, considerable vertical gain, picturesque surroundings, and a natural line of travel. The tour is described via the Chair Peak north slope descent, but should be done in the reverse direction in spring conditions. The described way offers nicer ski descents, but the reverse is less committing in questionable weather and lets you stay ahead of the sun later in the season.

**Approach:** Take Interstate 90 to the Snoqualmie Pass west exit. Drive on Alpental Road to the uppermost parking lot (3,220 feet).

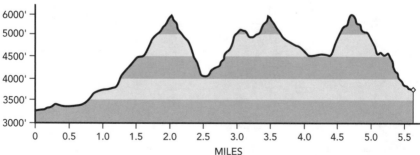

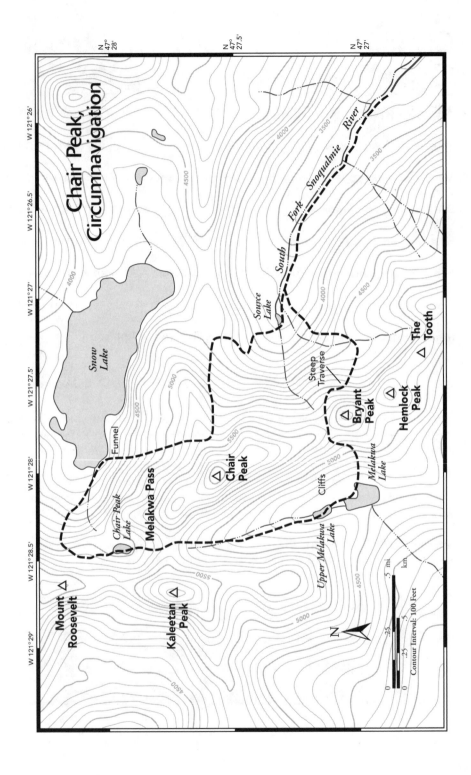

Chair Peak,
Circumnavigation

Snow Lake

Mount Roosevelt △

Kaleetan Peak △

Chair Peak Lake

Melakwa Pass

Funnel

Chair Peak △

Upper Melakwa Lake

Cliffs

Melakwa Lake

Bryant Peak △

Hemlock Peak △

The Tooth ◇

Steep Traverse

Source Lake

South Fork Snoqualmie River

N 47° 28'

N 47° 27.5'

N 47° 27'

W 121° 29'

W 121° 28.5'

W 121° 28'

W 121° 27.5'

W 121° 27'

W 121° 26.5'

W 121° 26'

N

.25    0    .5 mi

.25    0    .5    km

Contour Interval: 100 Feet

# Chair Peak, Circumnavigation

Chair Peak

Kaleetan Peak

Mt. Roosevelt
Tour

Upper Melakwa Valley from southeast. PHOTO BY SCOTT SCHELL

From the parking lot you'll see a groomed path leading deeper into the Alpental valley. Follow this path to its end. From here you continue up the valley, staying well above and south of the Snoqualmie River. Be aware that the north slopes of the valley are steep and very avalanche prone. Absolutely abandon this tour if snow stability is less than good. Once you reach Source Lake at 3,760 feet (1 hour to here), tour up the open slope that comes down from the Chair Peak basin. At around 4,300 feet start trending north toward a flat spot (4,450 feet). From here you have to ascend the steep slopes (going west) up into the Chair Peak basin.

The northern rim of the basin shows a very distinct notch (5,360 feet), which leads from the basin onto the north slopes below Chair Peak's spectacular north face. Climb from the basin into the notch (a short section of about 45- to 50-degree snow climbing and 2.5 hours to here). This is the first of the three 5,400-foot cols you'll pass.

Now start your ski descent to Snow Lake by skiing in a north-northwesterly direction until you come to the cliffs that form the western border of the north slope. The next section is a funnel for avalanches and needs to be assessed carefully. Ski down to the lake, staying close to the cliffs (4,016 feet; 3 to 3.5 hours to here).

From the lake, tour west to about 4,350 feet. The terrain steepens here; you'll have to swing north and then west again in order to gain the bench at

Melakwa Pass from the north. PHOTO BY MARTIN VOLKEN

5,000 feet below Mount Roosevelt. Tour past Chair Peak Lake and the spectacular east face of Kaleetan Peak to Melakwa Pass (5,350 feet; about 5 hours to here). This ascent is very scenic but quite committing in terms of avalanche potential.

From the pass ski down the beautiful little valley below the spectacular southwest flanks of Chair Peak to the Melakwa Lakes (4,500 feet; about 5.5 hours to here). Then tour in a northeasterly direction up the obvious slope below Bryant Peak. At 5,460 feet you'll reach a col located northwest of Bryant Peak (5,460 feet; about 6.5 hours to here). You're looking down into the Bryant Peak Couloir. This inviting 1,700-foot descent to Source Lake can be either a spectacular run or a very bad idea, since the couloir is a catch basin for the avalanches that occur higher up on the east slopes of the south shoulder. I've chosen to describe the other descent option. This is the more natural ascent line to the Bryant Peak col if you follow this tour in the reverse order.

From the col ski the entrance to the couloir for but a few turns, and start trending east immediately. Within 600 to 900 feet (200 to 300 meters), you'll arrive at a distinct shoulder below the north side of Bryant Peak's summit headwall. At about 5,100 feet turn south and ski down the steep but short slope into the Pineapple basin. Continue to the east side of the basin, then ski down through old hemlocks to the Source Lake area (3,760 feet; about 7 hours to here). From Source Lake ski along your ascent track out to the parking lot (3,220 feet; about 7.5 hours to here).

# Kaleetan Peak

*Tour 20*

**Tour distance:** 12 km (7.4 miles)

**Tour time:** 7 to 8 hours

**Vertical gain/loss:** 5,219 feet/5,219 feet

**Difficulty rating:** Grade III-plus

**Best season:** January through May

**Starting elevation/high point:** 3,220 feet/6,259 feet

**Gear required:** Standard ski-touring equipment, plus light ice ax and crampons

**Required fitness and skiing ability:** Very good fitness and very good skiing ability

**Map needed:** Snoqualmie Pass

Although it's the second highest and maybe most aesthetic peak in the immediate Snoqualmie Pass region, Kaleetan Peak is one of the least known. Kaleetan—which means "arrowhead"—describes the peak well. It features steep east and west faces and a very narrow, exposed north ridge. This ridge connects with Mount Roosevelt and makes for a great summer outing.

The triangular-shaped south face offers the only feasible ski descent. This descent off the exposed summit into the Melakwa valley is direct, steep, and beautiful.

**Approach:** Take Interstate 90 to the Snoqualmie Pass west exit. Drive on Alpental Road to the uppermost parking lot (3,220 feet).

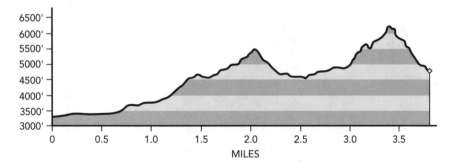

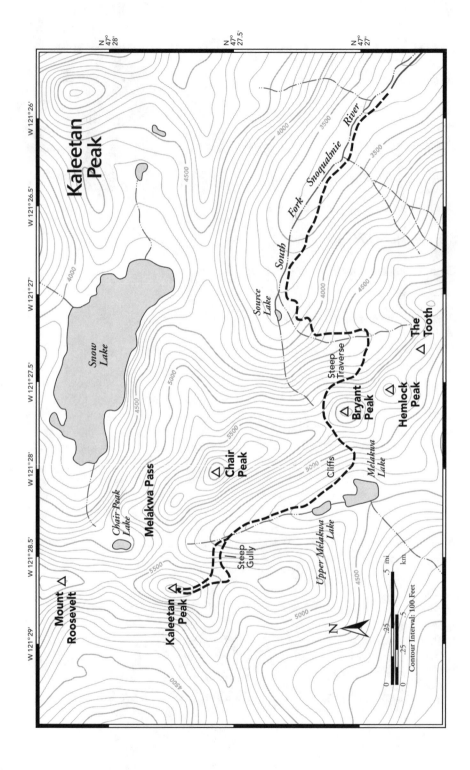

Kaleetan Peak

W 121°29'  W 121°28.5'  W 121°28'  W 121°27.5'  W 121°27'  W 121°26.5'  W 121°26'

N 47° 28'  N 47° 27.5'  N 47° 27'

Mount Roosevelt

Kaleetan Peak

Chair Peak Lake

Melakwa Pass

Snow Lake

Chair Peak

Steep Gully

Cliffs

Upper Melakwa Lake

Melakwa Lake

Bryant Peak

Steep Traverse

Hemlock Peak

The Tooth

Source Lake

South Fork Snoqualmie River

4000
3500
3500
4000
4500
4500
5000
5500
5500
5000
5000
4500
5500
5000
4500
4500
4000

N

0    .25    .5 mi
0  .25  .5  1 km

Contour Interval: 100 Feet

**Kaleetan Peak Tour**
Big Snow Mountain

Descent Option

To Gully

Kaleetan Peak from the southwest. PHOTO BY SCOTT SCHELL

From the parking lot you'll see a groomed path leading farther up the Alpental valley. Follow this path to its end, then continue up the valley well above and south of the Snoqualmie River. Be aware that the north slopes of the valley are steep and avalanche prone. Shortly before you reach Source Lake (3,760 feet; 1 hour to here), start touring in a southerly direction up the little tributary valley that leads to the Pineapple basin. Stay east of the drainage in big timber until you gain the upper, gentler portion of the valley (4,400 feet; about 2 hours to here).

Keep touring up the valley to 4,500 feet. Now turn west as if you were touring toward the east face of Bryant Peak. Turn northwest as the terrain steepens in front of you. As you face northwest you'll see a lightly treed shoulder between 4,800 and 5,000 feet. This is the only reasonable route around Bryant Peak. Be careful: This section of the tour is committing and demands solid judgment. Wrap around the shoulder and tour the short distance in a westerly direction to the Bryant Peak col (5,460 feet; about 3 hours to here).

From here ski down toward the Melakwa Lakes. If you trend too far to the right, you might find yourself on top of a cliff band in the 4,900-foot area. Once you reach the lakes, tour up the valley to about 4,900 feet. You'll see a steep but short east-facing gully that lets you reach a distinct notch between Kaleetan Peak and Point 5,700. Tour up to this notch (5,560 feet; about 4.5 hours to here). Then ski in a northerly direction for a short distance until you reach the south face of Kaleetan Peak at 5,600 feet. From here tour or climb to the summit, staying generally on the eastern edge of the face (6,259 feet; about 5.5 hours to here).

To descend, ski down the face to 5,600 feet. You can ski down the previously mentioned couloir or ski off the ridge in an easterly direction at the 5,750-foot level. This will get you directly to Melakwa Pass. It's a fun descent, but quite steep.

**Variation:** If you're behind schedule or conditions in the "very sunny" Melakwa valley have gotten too dangerous, you can finish the tour via Chair Peak Lake and Snow Lake. (A detailed description of this section can be found in Tour 19, Chair Peak Circumnavigation; you'll need to reverse the directions there.)

Ski down to the Melakwa Lakes and return to the Bryant Peak col (5,460 feet; about 7 hours to here). Be aware that the south-facing cliffs on Bryant Peak's southwest face hold snow and can trigger avalanches in a spring cycle.

From the col return to the Source Lake area via your ascent route (the inviting Bryant Peak Couloir can be a bad idea at this time of day). The couloir acts as a catch basin for the steep east face of Chair Peak's south shoulder.

From Source Lake return to your car via the ascent route (3,220 feet; about 8 hours to here).

# Mount Roosevelt

*Tour 21*

**Tour distance:** 10 km (6.2 miles)

**Tour time:** 6 to 8 hours

**Vertical gain/loss:** 3,548 feet/3,548 feet

**Difficulty rating:** Grade III

**Best season:** January through May

**Starting elevation/high point:** 3,220 feet/5,800 feet

**Gear required:** Standard ski-touring equipment

**Required fitness and skiing ability:** Very good physical fitness and advanced skiing ability

**Map needed:** Snoqualmie Pass

The view from the summit of Mount Roosevelt is probably the best in the area: You can see the complete Snoqualmie Haute Route (Tour 28), from start to finish. The tour itself offers a beautiful descent from the summit to Snow Lake. Timing is of the essence on this sun-exposed slope.

The trip can easily be combined with several others in the area, including Chair Peak Circumnavigation (Tour 19) and the North Slope Descent (Tour 17).

**Approach:** Take Interstate 90 to the Snoqualmie Pass west exit. Drive on Alpental Road to the uppermost parking lot (3,220 feet).

From the parking lot you'll see a groomed path leading deeper into the Alpental valley. Follow this path to its end. From here you continue up the valley, staying well above and south of the Snoqualmie River. Be aware that the

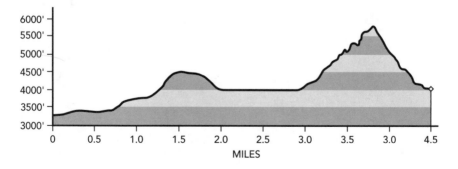

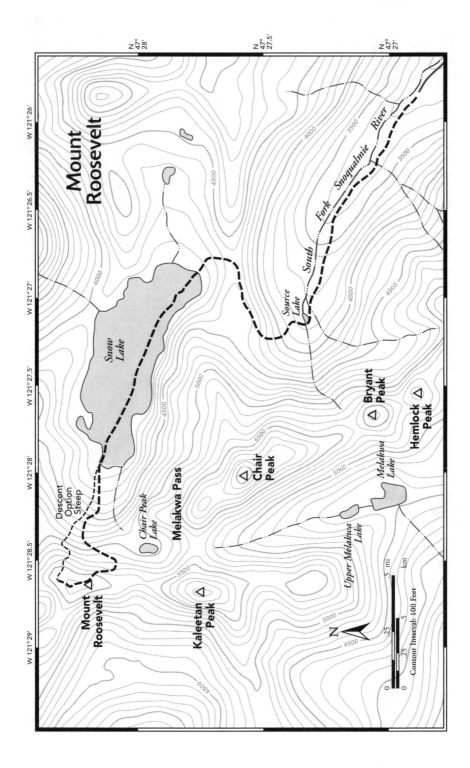

Mount Roosevelt from the east. PHOTO BY SCOTT SCHELL

north slopes of the valley are steep and very avalanche prone. Once you reach Source Lake at 3,760 feet (1 hour to here), tour up the open slope that comes down from the Chair Peak basin. At around 4,300 feet start trending north toward a flat spot (4,450 feet). You're now on Snow Lake Divide. Ski along the divide in a northeasterly direction until you reach an obvious pass that lets you ski down to Snow Lake (4,016 feet; 2 hours to here).

Cruise across the lake to its west end and start touring up in a westerly direction to about 4,350 feet. Here the terrain steepens; you'll have to swing north and then west again in order to gain the bench at 5,000 feet below Mount Roosevelt (3.5 to 4 hours to here). Now swing right and continue up in a north-northwesterly direction. At 5,400 feet the slope gets steep and demands great attention. You'll be under the Mount Roosevelt summit proper when you see a narrow, steep, but short draw. This will take you to a small plateau between two small summits north of Mount Roosevelt proper. Go to the notch between the summits and enjoy the spectacular view into a tributary drainage for Lower Wildcat Lake. The northernmost summit is the one clearly visible from Snow Lake Divide and the objective of the tour. Proceed the short distance from the notch to the summit by touring along the ridge in a northerly direction (5,800 feet; 4.5 to 5 hours to here).

To descend, you can of course retrace your ascent route. If conditions are good, you can also ski straight off the summit in an easterly direction. You must be certain of yourself. This descent is steep—between 5,400 and 5,000 feet—and should be done only in favorable conditions by an experienced skier. Continue down to the lake and return to the parking lot via the ascent route (3,220 feet; about 7 hours to here).

# Overnight Tours
## 22–26

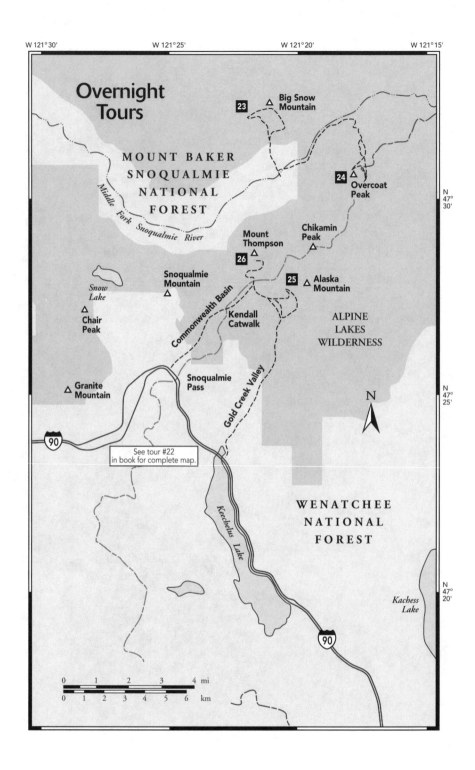

## Overnight Tours

# Jolly Mountain

**Tour distance:** 12 to 15 km (7 to 9 miles, depending on conditions on the forest road)

**Tour time:** 6 to 8 hours (depending on the condition of the forest road)

**Vertical gain/loss:** 3,000 to 4,000 feet (depending on conditions on the forest road)

**Difficulty rating:** Grade II

**Best season:** December through May

**High point:** 6,443 feet (the starting elevation will depend on the snow line)

**Gear required:** Standard ski-touring equipment

**Required fitness and skiing ability:** Good physical fitness and intermediate skiing ability

**Map needed:** Davis Peak

Jolly Mountain offers a nice alternative tour for the recreational skier who gets weathered out on Snoqualmie Pass. If you're already on the pass and it's raining (this hardly ever happens), simply keep driving and ski up this scenic peak. The views from the summit into the Stewart Range are spectacular. You'll also enjoy some great skiing in noncommitting terrain.

A look at the quick-info section above will tell you that the length of this tour depends heavily on the condition of the access road; in good conditions it can take you far up the lower reaches of Jolly Mountain. Learn more about

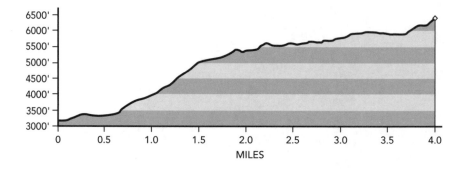

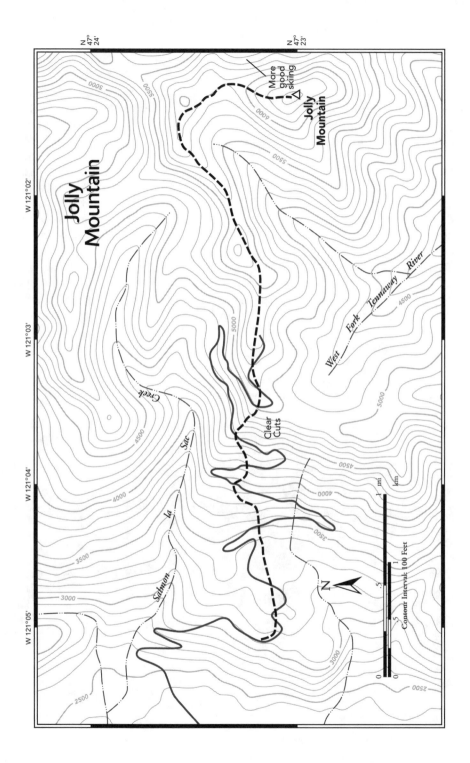

the road conditions and appropriate parking at the Cle Elum Ranger Station (509–674–4411).

**Approach:** Drive Interstate 90 to exit 80, then take Washington Highway 903 past Salmon La Sac. The turnoff to Forest Road 4315 is located about 1.5 miles north of the Red Mountain Campground. If you reach the Salmon La Sac Campground, you've gone about 1 mile too far. Go up FR 4315 as far as you can and park your car.

From your trailhead start touring up the hill in a generally easterly direction. The terrain will lead you through clear-cuts. If the snow cover is low, you might be better off touring up the forest road. At about 3,300 feet you'll come to a bigger flat spot. Continue touring in an easterly direction and start ascending steeper terrain. At about 4,600 feet the road starts winding around to the north. You can keep touring east, staying on a broad northwest-facing shoulder. At around 5,000 feet the road regains the shoulder.

The terrain is gentle from here. Follow the shoulder for about 3 kilometers (2 miles), first easterly and then northeasterly. You're now at the head of a cirque that faces southwest (5,900 feet). This cirque eventually drains into the West Fork of the Teanaway River. Stay on top of the ridge and turn south to gain the summit of Jolly Mountain (6,443 feet). Enjoy the view.

There's great skiing on the east side of the mountain down to about 5,000 feet.

To descend, return via your ascent route. Be careful: You're skiing through logging terrain, and stumps may be barely covered.

*Tour 22*

**Steve Gunderson near the summit of Jolly Mountain.**

*Photo by Andy Dappen*

# Big Snow Mountain

**Tour distance:** 15 km (9.3 miles)

**Tour time:** 5 to 6 hours

**Vertical gain/loss:** 3,670 feet/3,670 feet

**Difficulty rating:** Grade III+

**Best season:** April and May

**Starting elevation/high point:** 2,960 feet/6,650 feet

**Gear required:** Standard ski-touring equipment plus light ax and crampons for the variation, along with overnight equipment

**Required fitness and skiing ability:** Good physical fitness and advanced skiing ability (expert for the variation)

**Map needed:** Big Snow

The Big Snow Tour is a favorite of mine. It has a remote feel and a good amount of vertical, yet it can be done very safely. The views into the Lemah Range across the valley are alone worth the tour. You might want to call the North Bend Ranger District first for an update on Middle Fork Road conditions.

The tour is certainly doable as a day tour—but there's much good skiing to be had (see the variation), and the Hardscrabble basins with their fantastic granite are well worth seeing. You'll no doubt want to spend the night.

**Approach:** Take Interstate 90 to exit 34 just east of North Bend. Go north at the stop sign and drive past Ken's Truck Town. You'll reach the turnoff for

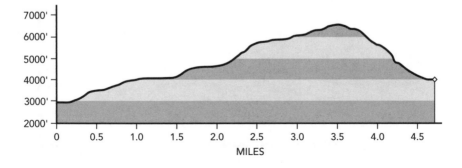

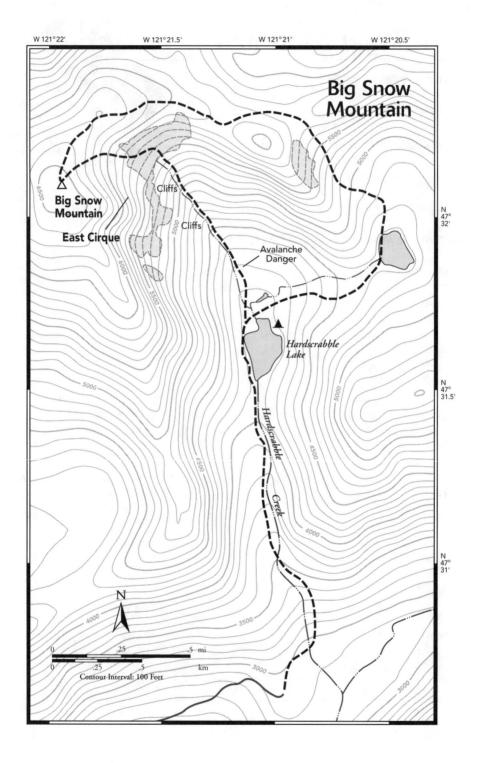

Big Snow Mountain

The author at Hardscrabble Lake. PHOTO JIM GRAHAM

Middle Fork of Snoqualmie Road just as the road starts to turn west. Get onto Middle Fork Road and proceed until it ends at a T intersection with a dirt road. This is Forest Road 56. Take a left onto FR 56 and drive for about 12 miles until you reach the turnoff for Forest Road 5640 just below the southwest face of Mount Garfield. Continue on FR 5640 for another 12 miles to the trailhead below Big Snow Mountain (2,960 feet). Park here. Please note that FR 5640 is a rough road that should be attempted only with a four-wheel-drive vehicle.

Start hiking or touring on the obvious trailhead that leads in a northeasterly direction deeper into the Middle Fork valley. After a short time of walking, you'll have to cross Hardscrabble Creek next to an old caved-in bridge. There may be a log crossing here.

Immediately after the crossing turn north and follow Hardscrabble Creek on its east side through what I'll call "Cascadian terrain." At about 3,500 feet you'll reach a bench that marks the entrance to a little hanging valley. Follow the valley until you reach Hardscrabble Lake at 4,059 feet (1 to 1.5 hours to here). The area on the southend of the lake has some great campsites. This will also put you in a great position for the variation the next day. You should find running water at the lake outflow.

After dropping off your camping gear, skirt the lake on its west side, turning east immediately after it to tour up the tributary drainage that leads to Upper Hardscrabble Lake at 4,594 feet. Please note that the landscape here is riddled with avalanche paths, although the touring itself is rather easy. The beautiful cirque that leads up from Lower Hardscrabble Lake to the summit ridge of Big Snow Mountain releases enormous slides every year and should be entered only in solid snow conditions.

From Upper Hardscrabble Lake keep skinning north-northwest up the steeper slope. It will lead you to a very distinct col at 5,800 feet (4 hours to here). Proceed up the simple but scenic summit ridge to the top of Big Snow Mountain at 6,650 feet (5 to 6 hours of touring to here).

From the summit return to your camp via your ascent track. Make sure to scope out the beautiful line that leads from the summit ridge down to Lower Hardscrabble Lake.

**Variation:** Ski the Big Snow south gully. This is a committing ski descent in a beautiful cirque. It would make an ideal tour if you're staying overnight. It's located directly north of Hardscrabble Lake. This line is steep enough that you probably want to climb it before you ski it. From your camp go to the north end of Hardscrabble Lake at 4,059 feet. Then climb (north) up to the drainage. A cliff band will flank your left (climber's left) until about 5,200 feet (about 1.5 hours to here).

Here the drainage opens up, and you'll find yourself on a steep, broad slope bordered by a 1,200-foot granite wall on climber's left. From the 5,400-foot level, start climbing west-northwest to the summit ridge at about 6,400 feet. Turn southwest and tour the short distance to the summit.

It's crucial to be on the summit early, so that you can choose the appropriate time for the descent. The entire Big Snow cirque has a southeast orientation and is prone to spring slide activity. The descent isn't what's considered extreme these days, but a fall in the upper portion of the slope could have dire consequences. Use your judgment! If the conditions in the cirque don't seem inviting enough for a direct descent, enjoy the descent down the summit ridge and Upper Hardscrabble Lake.

Once you're back at camp, return to the parking lot at the Middle Fork Trailhead via your ascent route from the previous day.

# Overcoat Peak

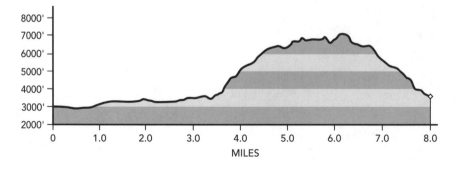

**Tour distance:** About 15 km (9.3 miles)

**Tour time:** 8 to 12 hours

**Vertical gain/loss:** 4,452 feet/4,452 feet

**Difficulty rating:** Grade III to IV

**Best season:** April and May

**Starting elevation/high point:** 2,960 feet/7,432 feet

**Gear required:** Overnight gear, ski-mountaineering gear, and a couple of pieces of medium-sized protection

**Required fitness and skiing ability:** Very good physical fitness and expert skiing ability

**Map needed:** Big Snow Mountain

Overcoat Peak is one of those peaks that make me feel lucky to live in this area. It's a great spot for introductory ski mountaineering and a good test route for bigger Cascadian high alpine ski tours. This little peak makes the transition into ski mountaineering—not because of gentle Overcoat Glacier, but rather because of its rugged-feeling summit area. Previous mountaineering experience is highly recommended if you want to go all the way to the summit. The combination of route finding, a river crossing, steep touring and skiing, and some climbing will let you appreciate this tour as a great adventure.

I've done the tour in a single day, but it certainly felt hasty. There's great skiing to be had in just about every direction from the beautiful Overcoat col; you'll want to take advantage of it with an overnight tour. Please keep in mind

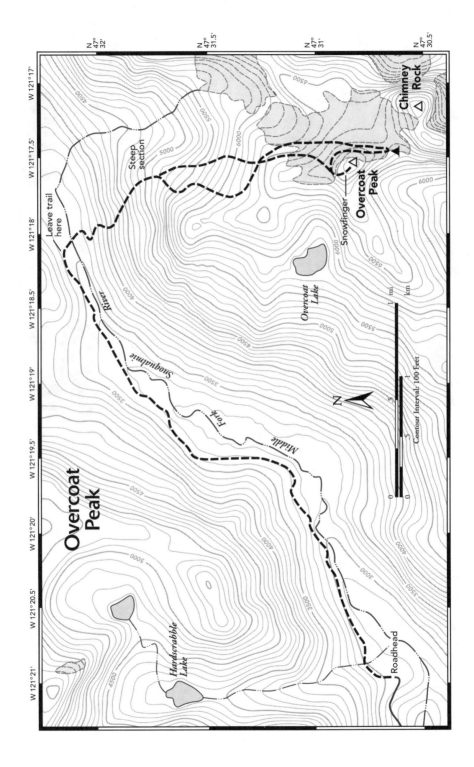

# Overcoat Peak

Chimney Rock

Overcoat Peak

Snowfinger

Overcoat Lake

Steep section

Leave trail here

River

Snoqualmie

Fork

Middle

Hardscrabble Lake

Roadhead

N

Contour Interval: 100 Feet

1 mi

km

N 47° 32'
N 47° 31.5'
N 47° 31'
N 47° 30.5'

W 121° 17'
W 121° 17.5'
W 121° 18'
W 121° 18.5'
W 121° 19'
W 121° 19.5'
W 121° 20'
W 121° 20.5'
W 121° 21'

4500
5000
5500
6000
6500
6000
6500
6000
5500
5000
4500
4000
3500
3000
3500
4000
4500
5000

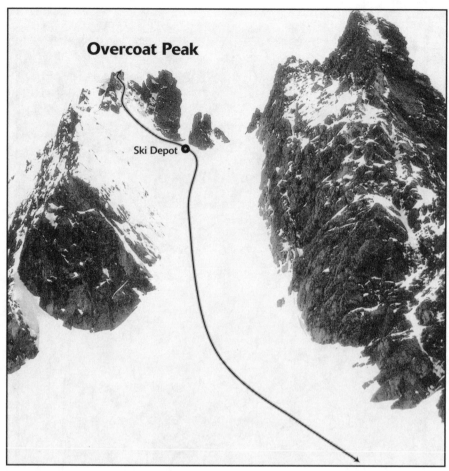

**Overcoat Peak**

Ski Depot ●

Overcoat Snowfinger from the north. PHOTO BY MARTIN VOLKEN

that the indicated travel times can vary greatly depending on your experience and ability level.

**Approach:** Take Interstate 90 to exit 34 just east of North Bend. Go north at the stop sign and drive past Ken's Truck Town. You'll reach the turnoff for Middle Fork of Snoqualmie Road just as the road starts to turn west. Get onto Middle Fork Road and proceed until it ends at a T intersection with a dirt road. This is Forest Road 56. Take a left onto FR 56 and drive for about 12 miles until you reach the turnoff for Forest Road 5640 just below the southwest face of Mount Garfield. Continue on FR 5640 for another 12 miles to the trailhead below Big Snow Mountain (2,960 feet). Park here. Please note that FR 5640 is a rough road that should be attempted only with a four-wheel-drive vehicle.

From the trailhead at the Middle Fork, ski or walk away from the parking lot in a northeasterly direction for about 600 feet (200 meters). You'll come to

Hardscrabble Creek and a log crossing by an old caved-in bridge. From here you can follow the Middle Fork hiking trail if it's visible; if not, follow the Middle Fork River upward, hugging the steep hillside but never getting more than 150 feet above the river. After about 5 kilometers (3.1 miles) you'll see a big, dark, steep 2,500-foot cliff on the south side of the river. This cliff appears to have a summit at the top, but this is merely the northernmost extension of a ridge that comes down from the Overcoat area.

Tour past this landmark cliff, and be sure to be at the river's edge at 3,520 feet (2 to 2.5 hours to here). On the south side of the river, you'll see a big open slope that steepens and narrows into a couloir. Cross the river. (It might be a good idea to bring one pair of water socks that can be tossed back and forth, since it's so easy to stub a toe in the cold water.) After this refreshing break, tour up the slope until it seems too inefficient to tour. Start climbing up the couloir to about 4,500 feet. Here the terrain steepens substantially. You need to assess the snow stability before climbing higher. Also, consider that this will be your ski descent.

**Variation:** If you don't feel good about the ascent, return to the river and continue to tour upstream until you find the distinct Overcoat drainage. Tour up the drainage, staying generally slightly right (west) of the drainage. The terrain steepens between 3,800 and 4,400 feet, but it remains tourable. From here tour straight south until you hit the lower lobe of Overcoat Glacier at about 5,600 feet. Then you can tour up the glacier to the Overcoat col at 6,800 feet. This col is located between Overcoat Peak and the Chimney Rock massif (3.5 to 4 hours from the river crossing spot, at 3,520 feet).

If you continue to climb the couloir, you'll probably have to carry your skis up the 5,000 feet. Here the terrain angles back and opens back up. Tour up this beautiful slope to the west of Overcoat Glacier in a south-southeasterly direction until you hit a gentle ridge at 6,200 feet. This ridge forms the western border of Overcoat Glacier (5 to 6 hours to here). From here tour the last section on the glacier straight south and past Overcoat Peak to the Overcoat col at 6,800 feet (7 hours to here). Camp here.

In the morning you can climb Overcoat Peak. It will add a sporty ski-mountaineering touch to this overnight tour. Break down camp and ski around Overcoat Peak counterclockwise until you come to the bottom of the north-facing snow finger.

Deposit unnecessary gear here and prepare for the ski-mountaineering portion of the tour. Climb up the snow finger carrying your skis; you can deposit them at the top of the finger. From here climb left up some likely snow-covered benches. After a couple of rope lengths, you'll come to a short but steep chimney. Climb this and continue to the summit ridge. Here you cross the ridge and follow the (very!) slabby ridge on its southwest side to the summit (7,432 feet; 2 hours to here). Reverse the ascent route for your descent. You'll find a good rappel block just when you cross back onto the north side of the ridge. One rappel will bring you to the mentioned ledges; then reverse your ascent route to your ski depot.

Andy Dappen pondering bridges.
Photo by Martin Volken

The ski descent from the top of the finger to the Middle Fork River is one of the nicest in the area.

The snow finger is short, but somewhat committing. From the bottom of the finger, ski in a north-northeasterly direction. This should bring you to the previously mentioned ridge, which borders Overcoat Glacier to the west (6,200 feet; 4 hours to here). From this point ski straight north and find the entrance to the couloir at 5,000 feet. If you ski too far west, you'll be stopped by the top of the previously noted landmark cliff. If you're too far to skier's right, you might end up in the Overcoat drainage (which is okay). From the entrance of the couloir, ski in a more or less northerly direction down to the river. Be careful: The entrance to the couloir is quite steep and needs to be assessed for stability (5 hours to here). If you don't feel good about it, opt for the Overcoat drainage.

You'll have to cross the river again and then follow your ascent route along the river back to the roadhead (7 hours to here).

# Alaska Mountain

**Tour distance:** 17 km (10.5 miles)

**Tour time:** 2 days

**Vertical gain/loss:** About 6,540 feet/6,540 feet

**Difficulty rating:** Grade III to IV

**Best season:** March through May

**Starting elevation/high point:** 2,980 feet/5,745 feet

**Gear required:** Standard ski-touring equipment plus light ice ax and crampons

**Required fitness and skiing ability:** Very good fitness and expert skiing ability

**Maps needed:** Snoqualmie Pass, Chikamin Peak

Along with Chikamin's southwest face, Alaska Mountain's south face may well be the most consistent long run in this region. With almost 2,600 feet of vertical, it's twice as long as the well-known Red Mountain west face. The top portion is quite steep (40 degrees plus), and the wide-open nature of the face adds to the exposure. Conditions for the approach and the descent need to be carefully evaluated: The route travels through steep south-facing terrain in spring. It's thus advisable to plan this outing as an overnight tour.

**Approach:** Take Interstate 90 to the Snoqualmie Pass west exit. Leave your car at the Summit West parking lot. Consider leaving a second car at the Hyak Ski Area (exit 53 off I–90).

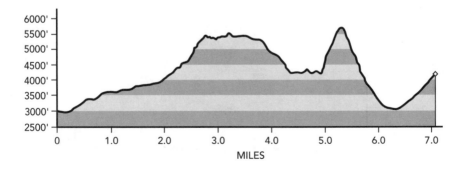

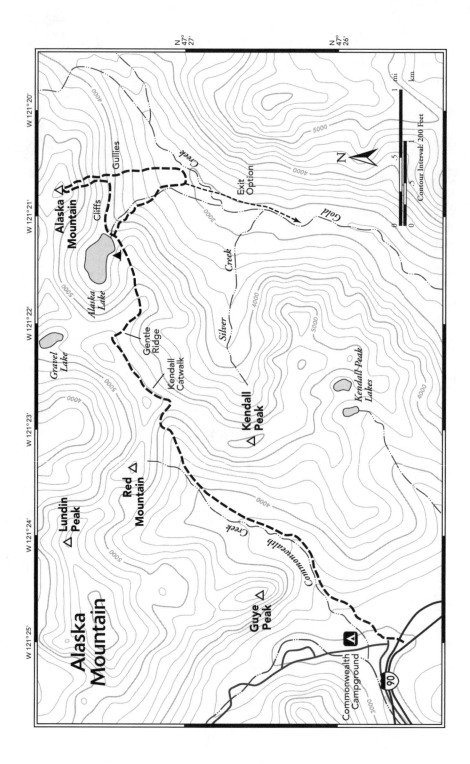

Alaska Mountain

N 47° 27'

N 47° 26'

W 121°20'  W 121°21'  W 121°22'  W 121°23'  W 121°24'  W 121°25'

Contour Interval: 200 Feet

N

1 mi

km

Alaska
Mountain

Gullies

Cliffs

Creek

Exit
Option

Gold

Silver

Creek

Alaska Lake

Gravel
Lake

Gentle
Ridge

Kendall
Catwalk

Kendall
Peak

Kendall Peak
Lakes

Lundin
Peak

Red
Mountain

Guye
Peak

Commonwealth

Creek

Commonwealth
Campground

90

Alaska Peak from the south. PHOTO BY SCOTT SCHELL

## Day 1

Follow the parking lot access road until it turns east—just a short distance. Turn left off the road and start touring up to the Commonwealth valley. Stay generally east of the creek until you reach a flat area next to Commonwealth Creek at around 3,560 feet. This is a key spot for many of the tours described. Up until the fall of 1999, there was a log crossing possibility at the flat spot. Depending on the depth of the snowpack, a crossing can be quite awkward here.

Remain on the east side of the creek and tour up the drainage between Red Mountain and Kendall Peak (3,900 feet; 2 hours to here). The pitch steepens at the headwall of the valley (4,600 feet). Gain the smaller upper basin on the north side of the valley (you may need to carry your skis here). Stay on the upper rim of this lightly forested area and head east until you gain the pass where the Pacific Crest Trail crosses (5,460 feet; 3.5 hours to here). You're now at the Kendall Catwalk. The trail—which has been blasted out of the slabby rock—may well be snow covered. Be careful. You also want to arrive early in the day, because the traverse catches a lot of morning sun and can be quite slide prone. If you don't feel good about the stability, climb up on the rocky crest to the north for about 300 feet. After the terrain angles back (about 5,600 feet), make a descending traverse to the 5,400-foot level and bypass the Kendall Catwalk. While the catwalk is sometimes easily passed, it can also cost you a few hours as you figure out a safe route around it.

Once you're past the catwalk, traverse northeast toward Ridge Lake (5,400 feet; about 4 hours to here). About 0.5 kilometer (0.3 mile) before Ridge Lake, you'll find a lightly treed ridge that trends away in a southeasterly direction (4 to 5 hours to here). Ski this ridge almost to its end at 5,350 feet. Now ski in a northeasterly direction to the outflow of Alaska Lake (4,500 feet; about 5 hours to here). You'll find good camping here.

**Variation:** It's important to get an early start on day 2, since you need to avoid a late traverse of the Kendall Catwalk on your way out. If this is a concern, you might want to camp down at Gold Creek and finish the tour via Gold Creek after your Alaska Mountain descent.

## Day 2

From Alaska Lake traverse in an easterly direction until you come to Alaska Mountain's southeast face. You will probably have to descend to around 4,000 feet. This is the easiest way to get around the westernmost rib to get onto the face proper. This is right about where the face starts to steepen; thorough snow-stability assessment here is crucial. If conditions don't seem quite right, absolutely abandon the descent. This face produces big avalanches.

If conditions are good, however, you can climb up to the summit (5,745 feet; about 3 hours to here).

The descent is straightforward. Assess the conditions well and enjoy the turns. Ski to about 3,200 feet and then return to your camp via the small drainage coming from Alaska Lake (4,500 feet; about 5 hours to here).

From Alaska Lake return to the Kendall Catwalk via your route from the previous day (5,400 feet; about 6 to 7 hours to here). Then traverse the catwalk and gain the saddle on its southern end. From here you can ski down to the Commonwealth drainage and out to Snoqualmie Pass via your ascent route (2,980 feet; about 8 to 9 hours to here).

**Variation:** If the catwalk crossing seems too dangerous, you can traverse above the catwalk at 5,600 feet on gentler ground until you hit a south-trending ridge. (This was also described for the approach.) A few hundred feet of simple but exposed scrambling will bring you back to the col south of the Kendall Catwalk.

# Mount Thompson

*Tour 26*

**Tour distance:** 20 km (12.4 miles)

**Tour time:** 2 days

**Vertical gain/loss:** 5,100 feet/5,300 feet

**Difficulty rating:** Grade IV

**Best season:** February through May

**Starting elevation/high point:** 2,980 feet/6,554 feet

**Gear required:** Ski-mountaineering equipment and overnight gear plus a few pieces of rock climbing protection

**Required fitness and skiing ability:** Very good physical fitness and expert skiing ability; mountaineering experience is recommended

**Maps needed:** Snoqualmie Pass, Chikamin Peak

The Mount Thompson Tour is a good introduction to Cascade ski mountaineering. This tour is serious and remains challenging long after you've come off Mount Thompson.

If you've ever skied at Alpental, you've probably noticed the distinct "Black Tusk" feature to the north. Mount Thompson is a fantastic summit because of its exposure, remote feel, and excellent views into the Lemah area. Anyone who climbs it should have knowledge in basic snow and rock climbing and advanced snow-stability evaluation skills.

**Approach:** Take Interstate 90 to the Snoqualmie Pass west exit. Leave your vehicle at the Summit West parking lot. It might be worthwhile to leave another car

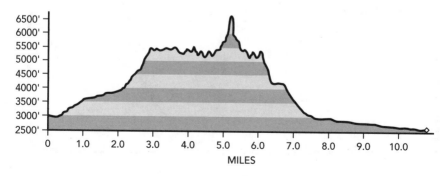

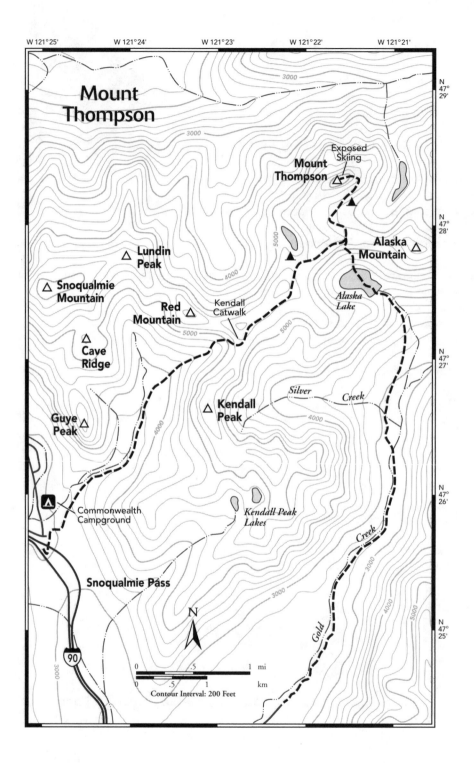

W 121°25'    W 121°24'    W 121°23'    W 121°22'    W 121°21'

# Mount Thompson

3000

3000

Exposed
Skiing

**Mount
Thompson** △

△ **Lundin
Peak**

△ **Snoqualmie
Mountain**

**Alaska
Mountain** △

**Red
Mountain** △

Kendall
Catwalk

*Alaska
Lake*

△ **Cave
Ridge**

5000

*Silver    Creek*

**Guye
Peak** △

△ **Kendall
Peak**

4000

▲ **Commonwealth
Campground**

*Kendall Peak
Lakes*

*Creek*

3000

**Snoqualmie Pass**

3000

N

*Gold*

0        .5        1  mi

0      .5      1    km

Contour Interval: 200 Feet

90

N
47°
29'

N
47°
28'

N
47°
27'

N
47°
26'

N
47°
25'

Ski Depot

Mount Thompson

The original Snoqualmie Haute Route crew in the Thompson basin; from left Volken, Avolio, Hattrup, and Dappen. PHOTO CARL SKOOG

at the Hyak Ski Area (exit 53 off I–90), since the second day of this tour is quite long.

## Day 1

Follow the parking lot access road until it turns east—just a short distance. Turn left off the road and start touring up to the Commonwealth valley. Stay generally east of the creek until you reach a flat area next to Commonwealth Creek at around 3,560 feet. This is a key spot for many of the tours described. Up until the fall of 1999, there was a log crossing possibility at the flat spot. Depending on the depth of the snowpack, a crossing can be quite awkward here.

Stay on the east side of the creek and tour until you enter the tributary valley between Red Mountain and Kendall Peak (3,900 feet; 2 hours to here). When you come to the headwall of the valley, it steepens substantially (4,600 feet). Go to the north side of the valley and gain the smaller upper basin. (You might need to carry your skis here.) Stay on the upper rim of the lightly forested area and tour to the east until you gain the pass where the Pacific Crest Trail crosses (5,460 feet; about 3.5 hours to here).

You're now at the entrance to the Kendall Catwalk. Chances are that the trail—which was blasted out of the slabby rock wall—is snow covered. Be careful here. It's important to arrive at this point fairly early, since the following traverse has the perfect angle and exposure for spring slide danger. If you don't feel good about the stability, you can climb up on the rocky crest to the north for about 300 feet (100 meters). Then the terrain angles back at about 5,700 feet, and you should be able to traverse above the Kendall Catwalk in a slight descent until you reach the 5,400-foot level again. This little section can be very easy or it could cost you a couple of hours, depending on the shape of the catwalk.

Once you're past the catwalk and on the 5,400-foot level, traverse in a northeasterly direction to Ridge Lake (4.5 hours to here).

The following traverse above Alaska Lake can be called dangerous, considering that you'll probably reach it in the middle of the afternoon. You must assess its stability before committing to the traverse. This steep traverse above the cliffs by Alaska Lake is east-southeast facing and not a spot for snow-stability gambling. You may be better advised to make camp at Rachel Lake and traverse early in the morning. After about 0.5 kilometer (0.3 mile) of traversing at 5,200 feet, turn uphill (north) and gain a distinct pass (Bumblebee Pass, 5,400 feet). From here ski down to the beautiful Thompson basin and camp (6 to 8 hours to here).

If the Alaska Lake traverse seems like a bad option, you can traverse north from Ridge Lake until you're above Gravel Lake. Then turn east and up the steep slopes to the west saddle of the Thompson basin (5,780 feet). From here ski down into the basin and reach camp (also 6 to 8 hours to here).

## Day 2

It's crucial to get onto the east flank of Thompson at first daylight. Do so by touring up the obvious ramp to the first bench at the bottom of the east flank (5,700 feet). Depending on conditions, you'll want to carry your skis up the 6,100-foot area and stash them. From here rope, crampons, and some protection might be needed. There's some exposure toward the summit, which can best be reached by traversing toward the south face once you reach the summit block. From here a short climb in the upper third-class terrain will let you top out. The east ridge of Mount Thompson is a basic route in summer, but you'll most likely encounter more challenging conditions, since the mountain will probably present itself in a late-winter cloth (6,554 feet; 2 to 4 hours to here).

To descend, reverse your ascent route back to camp. The slope is skiable from about 6,100 feet but needs to be judged very carefully. There are a few very steep rollers that could release. Furthermore, don't forget to stay ahead of the sun: This slope gets sun very early (4 to 5 hours to here).

From camp tour up the short but steep slope to Bumblebee Pass (5,400 feet). Switch to ski mode here and ski straight south down the narrow couloir to Alaska Lake. This chute could be riddled with avalanche debris; it's about

40 degrees. This rowdy descent (on skis or on foot) will bring you right to the edge of Avalanche Lake (4,200 feet; about 6 hours to here).

It might be tedious and dangerous trying to traverse along the banks of the lake. Unless the lake isn't in shape, rope up in your best glacier ski-touring fashion and scoot right across it in a southeasterly direction. From the outflow continue to drop down to the Gold Creek valley in a southeasterly direction. Follow on the west side of the Alaska Lake drainage to about 3,600 feet. From here descend in a more southerly direction all the way to the valley bottom at 3,000 feet.

Stay on the west side of Gold Creek until you're about 0.25 mile south of the small Silver Creek drainage. You should find a crossing here to get to the east side of Gold Creek (about 7 to 8 hours to here). All that remains is the long but scenic 6-kilometer (3.7 mile) scoot to the I–90 corridor.

Stay on the east side of Gold Creek until you hit the road for the Hyak development at around 2,660 feet. The last 2 kilometers (1.2 miles) follow this road to I–90 (9 to 10 hours to here).

*Tour 26*
**Mt. Thompson from the south.**
*Photo by Martin Volken*

# Multiday Tours
## 27-28

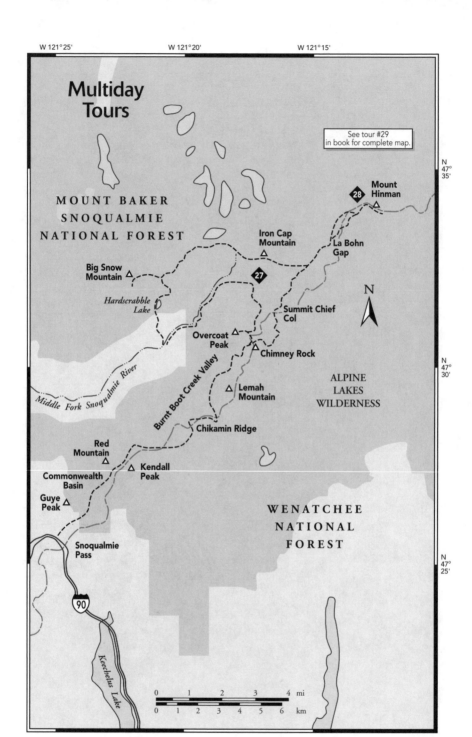

# Multiday Tours

See tour #29 in book for complete map.

N 47° 35'

**28** Mount Hinman

MOUNT BAKER
SNOQUALMIE
NATIONAL FOREST

Iron Cap Mountain

La Bohn Gap

Big Snow Mountain

**27**

*Hardscrabble Lake*

N

Summit Chief Col

Overcoat Peak

Chimney Rock

*Burnt Boot Creek Valley*

*Middle Fork Snoqualmie River*

Lemah Mountain

ALPINE
LAKES
WILDERNESS

N 47° 30'

Chikamin Ridge

Red Mountain

Kendall Peak

Commonwealth Basin

Guye Peak

WENATCHEE

NATIONAL

FOREST

N 47° 25'

Snoqualmie Pass

**90**

*Keechelus Lake*

0    1    2    3    4  mi
0  1  2  3  4  5  6  km

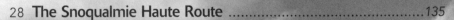

## Multiday Tours

*Tour 28, Day 4*
**Heading toward Summit
Chief Col.**

*Photo by Carl Skoog*

# The Little Snoqualmie Haute Route

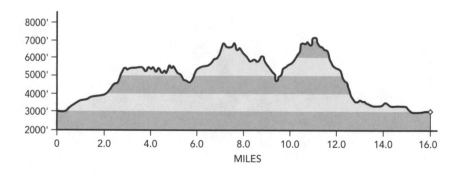

**Tour distance:** 28 to 30 km (17.4 to 18.6 miles)

**Tour time:** 3 days

**Vertical gain/loss:** About 11,000 feet/11,000 feet, depending on your variation

**Difficulty rating:** Grade IV

**Best season:** March through May

**Starting elevation/high point:** 2,980 feet/7,432 feet

**Gear required:** Standard ski-mountaineering equipment and overnight gear

**Required fitness and skiing ability:** Excellent fitness and expert skiing ability

**Maps needed:** Snoqualmie Pass, Chikamin Peak, Big Snow

The Little Snoqualmie Haute Route isn't that little. It takes you through the immediate backcountry north of Snoqualmie Pass and uses Overcoat Glacier as a turnaround point. The route is committing and physically challenging; it demands sound judgment. The tour can be done from both ends and follows the Snoqualmie Haute Route (Tour 28) for a good part of the way. Tour 28 is described from the Middle Fork; this route is detailed from Snoqualmie Pass. This description should also serve if you want to complete the Snoqualmie Haute Route from the pass, since the section described is probably the trickiest in terms of timing and route finding. After you complete this tour, your view

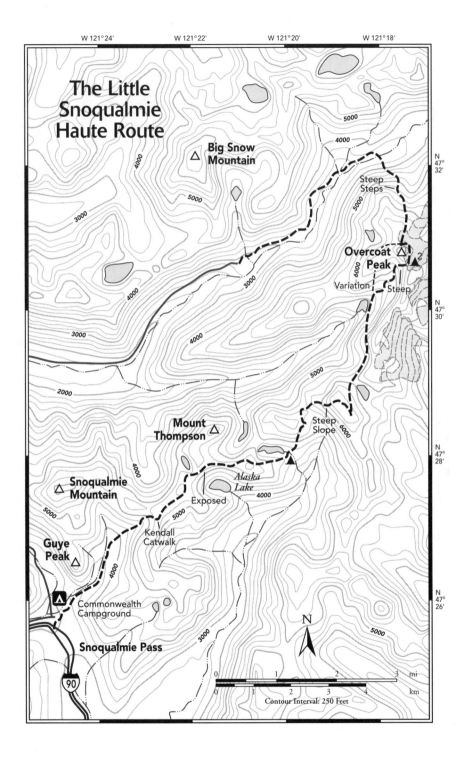

The Little Snoqualmie Haute Route

W 121°24'    W 121°22'    W 121°20'    W 121°18'

N 47°32'
N 47°30'
N 47°28'
N 47°26'

Big Snow Mountain

Steep Steps

Overcoat Peak

Variation    Steep

Steep Slope

Mount Thompson

Alaska Lake

Exposed

Snoqualmie Mountain

Kendall Catwalk

Guye Peak

Commonwealth Campground

Snoqualmie Pass

90

N

0        1        2        3   mi
0    1    2    3    4   km
Contour Interval: 250 Feet

from the top of the Alpental Ski Area into the Snoqualmie Pass backcountry will be changed forever—I promise.

**Approach:** Take Interstate 90 to the Snoqualmie Pass west exit. Leave your car at the Summit West Ski Area parking lot. Start here. It's advisable to park another car at the end of Middle Fork Road. Please refer to the Approach section of Tour 28.

# Day 1

Go up Alpental Road for about 300 feet to the turnoff for the Commonwealth basin parking lot. Turn north here and follow the valley well east of Commonwealth Creek. You'll come close to the creek at the flat spot at around 3,560 feet. Stay east of the creek and keep touring up the valley for about 1.5 kilometers (0.9 mile) past the west flanks of Kendall Peak.

At about 3,850 feet you'll run into the tributary stream that drains into Commonwealth Creek from the basin between Red Mountain and Kendall Peak. Head into this drainage, staying to the right (south) of the tributary stream to about 4,600 feet. Here the terrain steepens; you're best off touring to the left out of the trees and then making a sweeping right turn to the col at 5,400 feet (3 hours to here).

At this pass you should see the famous Kendall Catwalk traversing the steep southeast flank above Silver Creek in a northeasterly direction. If you can't see this obvious catwalk, which has been blasted out of the rock, it may be snow covered—or you may be off route. Do not attempt to tour across the slope unless you're absolutely sure of its stability. You may be better off climbing up the short rocky ridge to the north for about 200 feet. Here the flank angles back quite a bit, and you can tour again in a northeasterly direction, remaining at about 5,500 feet. You'll get to Ridge Lake after about 1.5 kilometers (0.9 mile). This little lake makes a second key spot on the tour.

If it's early in the day and conditions are good, you can keep traversing, maintaining the same elevation across the exposed slopes high above Alaska Lake then on to the saddle at the base west of Alaska Mountain (5,350 feet; 5 hours to here).

If the traverse seems unsafe, turn north for a short distance from Ridge Lake to the east side of Gravel Lake. Turn east and ascend the steep slopes to the west entrance of the Thompson basin. This entrance consists of a gentle but mostly corniced saddle. You should find good ways into the basin on the south end or the north end of the saddle just south of the distinct ridge of small towers. From the entrance ski into the beautiful basin and stay on the south side of it. About 0.75 kilometer (0.5 mile) from the entrance, you'll see a distinct col on the southern rim of the basin. This is Bumblebee Pass (5,400 feet). Ascend the slope to the col, drop to the other side to about 5,400 feet, and regain the previously mentioned traverse to the Alaska Mountain saddle (6 hours to here).

Please keep in mind that both of these options harbor significant avalanche dangers. Timing is key.

From this saddle climb the steep but wooded slopes to Alaska Mountain's north summit area. Right at this point you can drop off the summit to the gentler northwest side. In a descending traverse ski under the summit in a southeasterly direction until you come to the wooded west ridge of Alaska Mountain, at around 5,400 feet. From here enjoy a simple ski descent through virgin timber to Joe Lake at 4,624 feet (about 7 to 8 hours to here). Camp here. You should be able to find running water at the lake outflow.

## Day 2

It's crucial to get an early start, since the slopes to Chikamin Ridge are steep, long, and south facing. From your camp at the east end of Joe Lake, tour north on the eastern edge of Huckleberry Mountain's south face. At around 5,100 feet you'll be able to wrap around to the eastern side of the mountain. Keep touring north onto a bench that becomes very distinct and wide at about 5,350 feet. Pass Point 5,524 on the map to the west and continue for another 900 feet (300 meters) until you come to the gentle saddle that connects Huckleberry Mountain and Chikamin Ridge (1 hour to here).

Turn northeast and follow this saddle until you get to the far northwestern extension of Chikamin's flank. At about 5,700 feet turn east and start making a rising traverse up the steep flank of Chikamin Ridge. Gain Chikamin Ridge by touring up (or climbing up) the northwestern part of its southwest flank. You'll reach the ridge about 600 feet (200 meters) southeast of Point 6,920 on the map. Make sure not to get drawn too far to the southeast while climbing the flank (2.5 to 3 hours to here).

From the ridge ski in a southeasterly direction until you're just north and below the summit gully of Chikamin Peak, at 6,800 feet. Then ascend the gully to the summit col. This saddle may be corniced, making the final ascent from the col up the summit blocks to climber's right quite difficult. If conditions allow it, Chikamin Peak (7,000 feet) is a worthwhile summit on the way. There's a fantastic viewpoint in the middle of the traverse. Still, although the ascent is short and not technical, you must remain cautious: The gully is steep and will harbor a lot of wind-deposited snow. The cornice may be difficult to navigate, and the summit blocks aren't all that solid. Consider the time of day. You may want to forgo the summit in order to get to camp safely.

Upon returning to your ski depot (4 hours to here) at the bottom of the gully, start skiing straight north past the south end of Chikamin Lake, at 5,600 feet. This will situate you just west of the southernmost Lemah Tower. From here you have to ascend the short distance to the col east of Point 6,022 on the map (5,920 feet; 6 hours to here).

The next ski descent from the col to Iceberg Lake is easy, beautiful, and spectacular. The looming walls of the Lemah Towers are steep but hold a surprising amount of snow in classic Cascade fashion. Be aware that the spectacular upper Burntboot Creek valley can be a very dangerous spot to be.

Skirt Iceberg Lake on its east side and start touring in a northeasterly direction up the valley. You'll tour right up toward the southwest face of Overcoat

## Little Snoqualmie Haute Route
### Day 2

Overcoat Peak       Chimney Rock

Variation

Lemah Group and Burntboot Creek Valley from southwest. PHOTO BY SCOTT SCHELL

Peak. At around 6,200 feet turn east and then northeast again to climb the steep slope leading up to the Overcoat col. Camp here (6,800 feet; 8 to 9 hours to here).

Conditions vary on this slope from year to year, but you may find easy snow climbing on the northern edge of the slope (climber's left).

**Variation:** The final slope up to the Overcoat col is steep, and you've been touring for about 8 hours already. If you don't feel good about the conditions on this slope, you can start touring in a northerly direction from 5,600 feet up the southern slopes of the Burntboot Creek valley. This will put you on the ridge due west of Overcoat Peak. This is a good campsite as well. The views into the towers are outrageous. From here you circumnavigate Overcoat Peak clockwise, maintaining about the same elevation. You'll eventually reach Overcoat Glacier north of Overcoat Peak and hook back up with the route.

### Day 3

The next morning you can climb Overcoat Peak. It will add a sporty ski-mountaineering touch to this overnight tour.

Break down camp and ski around Overcoat Peak counterclockwise until you come to the bottom of the north-facing snow finger.

Deposit unnecessary gear here and prepare for the ski-mountaineering portion of the tour. Carry your skis up the snow finger and deposit them at the top. Then climb left up some likely snow-covered benches. After a couple of rope lengths, you'll come to a short but steep chimney. Climb this and proceed up to the summit ridge. Here you'll cross the ridge and follow the (very!) slabby ridge on its southwest side to the summit (7,432 feet; 2 hours to here).

Reverse the ascent route for your descent. There's a good rappel block just at the spot where you cross back onto the north side of the ridge. One rappel will bring you back to the mentioned ledges. From here reverse your ascent route back to your ski depot.

If you're not planning to climb Overcoat Peak, you can get a bit of a later start and enjoy the remote feel of the Lemah–Chimney Rock Wilderness.

From camp you ski in a north-northeasterly direction down Overcoat Glacier and drainage to the Middle Fork River at 3,500 feet (1 hour respectively 4 hours to here). You'll then have to cross the Middle Fork River. No fancy solutions here. Find a safe crossing and revel in the knowledge that anyone can walk across a bridge.

**Variation:** If you're a more committed skier, you can ski from the top of the Overcoat snow finger (about 45 to 50 degrees at the top) in a more straight northerly direction. This descent is sportier and trickier to find; it demands more judgment of snow stability. If completed, it will save you about 1 kilometer (0.6 mile) of scooting along the Snoqualmie Middle Fork.

The ski descent from the top of the finger to the Middle Fork River is one of the nicest in the area. It's short, but somewhat committing. From the bottom of the finger, ski in a north-northeasterly direction. This should bring you to the previously mentioned ridge, which borders Overcoat Glacier to the west (6,200 feet; about 4 hours to here). From this point ski straight north and find the entrance to a couloir at 5,000 feet. If you ski too far to the west, you'll be stopped by the top of a big cliff that reaches all the way to the floor of the Middle Fork valley. If you're too far to skier's right, you might end up in the Overcoat drainage (which is okay). From the entrance to the couloir, ski in a more or less northerly direction down to the river. Be careful: The entrance to the couloir is quite steep and needs to be assessed for stability (5 hours to here). If you don't feel good about it, opt for the Overcoat drainage.

You'll have to cross the river here and regain the described route along the north side of the Middle Fork River.

On the other side of the river, ascend to about 3,600 feet. You should find signs of the Middle Fork Hiking Trail. If the trail is still snow covered, follow the river downstream, staying always between 50 and 150 vertical feet above the river. You'll come across the Crawford Creek drainage after about 1.5 kilometers (0.9 mile) and the Hardscrabble Creek drainage after about 5 kilometers (3.1 miles). The Hardscrabble Creek drainage might be a bit more problematic to cross during a spring runoff, but right next to an old caved-in bridge at about 2,960 feet you should find possibilities for a crossing—perhaps a log. You're now a couple of hundred yards from the roadhead (4 hours to here; 8 hours if you climbed the Overcoat summit).

Please keep in mind that the time estimate for the third day stops at the end of Middle Fork Road. You may need to ski or walk out along the road for a while, depending on road conditions. Actual driving time from the roadhead to North Bend is about 1.5 hours.

# The Snoqualmie Haute Route

*Tour 28*

**Tour distance:** About 65 km (40.3 miles), depending on your variation

**Tour time:** 5 to 6 days

**Vertical gain/loss:** About 20,000 feet (depending on your variation)

**Difficulty rating:** Grade IV to V

**Best season:** March through June

**Starting elevation/high point:** 2,960 feet (at Middle Fork of Snoqualmie Roadhead)/7,495 feet (at Mount Hinman)

**Gear required:** Standard overnight ski-touring equipment plus crampons, ice ax, some rescue gear, and a light rope

**Required fitness and skiing ability:** Excellent physical condition and expert skiing ability

**Maps needed:** Big Snow Mountain, Mount Daniel, Chikamin Peak, Snoqualmie Pass

The Snoqualmie Haute Route is a multiday tour that draws the most out of the Snoqualmie Pass region's hinterlands. The area has an amazingly rugged character, and this tour must be considered very committing. Although the glacial element is missing for the most part, this is more difficult than many a high

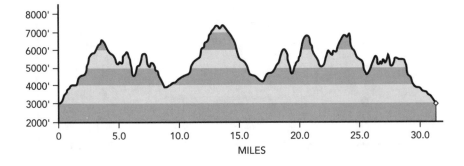

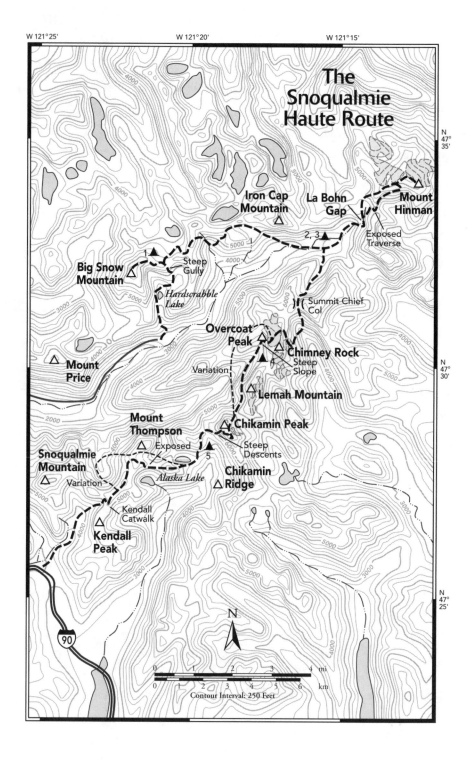

The
Snoqualmie
Haute Route

W 121°25'    W 121°20'    W 121°15'

N 47° 35'

N 47° 30'

N 47° 25'

Iron Cap Mountain

La Bohn Gap

Mount Hinman

2, 3

Exposed Traverse

Big Snow Mountain

Steep Gully

Hardscrabble Lake

Summit Chief Col

Overcoat Peak

Chimney Rock

Steep Slope

Mount Price

Variation

4

Lemah Mountain

Mount Thompson

Chikamin Peak

Snoqualmie Mountain

Exposed

5

Steep Descents

Variation

Alaska Lake

Chikamin Ridge

Kendall Catwalk

Kendall Peak

90

N

0    1    2    3    4 mi
0  1  2  3  4  5  6  km

Contour Interval: 250 Feet

alpine tour I've completed in the region. The terrain is wildly scenic, the skiing is challenging, navigation is demanding, and the total vertical gain is taxing. Still, you're never more than 24 kilometers (15 miles) from Snoqualmie Pass.

**Approach:** Take Interstate 90 to exit 34 just east of North Bend. Go north at the stop sign and drive past Ken's Truck Town. You'll reach the turn off for Middle Fork of Snoqualmie Road just as the road starts to turn west. Get onto Middle Fork Road and proceed until it ends at a T intersection with a dirt road. This is Forest Road 56. Take a left onto FR 56 and drive for about 12 miles until you reach the turnoff for Forest Road 5640 just below the southwest face of Mount Garfield. Continue on FR 5640 for another 12 miles to the trailhead below Big Snow Mountain (2,960 feet). Park here. Please note that FR 5640 is a rough road that should be attempted only with a four-wheel-drive vehicle.

The Snoqualmie Haute Route is certainly doable from both ends (the Commonwealth basin and Middle Fork Roadhead), but the following route description leaves you more options if conditions become questionable. It's much easier to get shut down by poor snow conditions or bad weather if you start this tour from Snoqualmie Pass. Still, if the conditions are favorable and the access on Middle Fork Road isn't that good, a start from Snoqualmie Pass may well be your simplest option. You can leave a vehicle toward Middle Fork Roadhead before the trip. Cell phone coverage is actually quite good on the whole tour, so you can also plan for someone to come and pick you up.

## Day 1

Start hiking or touring on the obvious trailhead that leads in a northeasterly direction deeper into the Middle Fork valley. After a short time of walking, you'll have to cross Hardscrabble Creek bridge. Immediately after the crossing follow the drainage up Hardscrabble Creek through what I'll call "Cascadian terrain." At about 3,500 feet you'll reach a bench that marks the beginning of the upper portion of a little hanging valley. Tour up the valley until you reach Hardscrabble Lake at 4,059 feet (1 to 1.5 hours to here).

Skirt the lake on its west side, turning east immediately after it to tour up the tributary drainage that leads to Upper Hardscrabble Lake at 4,594 feet. Please note that the landscape here is riddled with avalanche paths, although the touring itself is rather easy. The beautiful cirque that leads up from Lower Hardscrabble Lake to the summit ridge of Big Snow Mountain releases enormous slides every year and should be entered only in solid snow conditions.

From Upper Hardscrabble Lake keep skinning north-northwest up the steeper slope. It will lead you to a very distinct col at 5,800 feet (4 hours to here). This makes an excellent campsite. After establishing camp proceed up the simple but scenic summit ridge to the top of Big Snow Mountain at 6,650 feet (5 to 6 hours of touring to here).

From the summit you can return to camp via your ascent track on the summit ridge.

## Day 2

From the 5,800-foot col ski down in a northeasterly direction toward Gold Lake. At about 5,600 feet you'll encounter a steep slope, which you should assess for stability. Ski down the steep slope hugging the cliffs on your right until you reach the 5,300-foot elevation. Watch out for hidden glide cracks. Now start touring uphill, still going in a northeasterly direction. (You're leaving the small Gold Lake drainage.) At 5,400 feet you'll reach a gentle shoulder that lets you enter a small, unnamed basin. Cross this basin in an easterly direction and tour up the steep slopes to a pass at 6,000 feet. The ridge you're standing on divides the north-draining Gold Lake basins from the south-draining Crawford Creek.

**Variation:** If the ascent slope to the 6,000-foot pass seems unsafe, you can tour up the basin in a counterclockwise fashion. An upper bench scribes the whole basin. This bench is very easily accessed from the basin's southwestern area. You'll reach the shelf at about 5,700 feet and stay on it while touring counterclockwise. This way you'll reach the relatively gentle slope that leads up to the pass.

From the pass make a north-northeasterly trending descent to the Crawford Creek drainage. Follow this drainage down to about 4,300 feet, then skin back up the steep tributary drainage in a northeasterly direction. At 5,200 feet you'll reach a small basin. Turn north here and tour up to the ridge crest that situates you directly north of Chetwood Lake. Follow the ridge to the east and reach the skin-off point within 900 feet (300 meters).

From this high point at 5,750 feet, ski down, skirting Crawford Lake to the north. If conditions are good, you can traverse as far east as possible and reach the valley floor of the Middle Fork of the Snoqualmie by traversing under the southern slopes of Iron Cap Mountain. There are tremendous gullies emptying out from Iron Cap's summit area. These gullies would make for some fun ski descents, but they present a sizable hazard, especially later in the day. If the avalanche risk is too high, you're better off following one of the drainages from Crawford Lake and reaching the Middle Fork valley floor a little farther west.

From your current location at about 3,900 feet, tour about 2 kilometers (1.2 miles) to the 4,100-foot level. There are many good campsite here, and you're in an ideal position for further touring toward Mount Hinman or Summit Chief Mountain.

## Day 3

This is a great day, because you're carrying only a day pack. You'll return to the same camp after your ascent of Mount Hinman. From your camp you can reach the headwaters of the Middle Fork very easily by touring to the east. You should reach Williams Lake within an hour. Pass Williams Lake on its south, then turn north immediately after it. The gentle bench will let you reach Chain Lakes very easily, though it's exposed to the slabby rock wall on tourer's right. Once you're at Chain Lakes, turn east and tour up the steep slopes to La Bohn Gap at 6,100 feet. From here traverse the steep cirque above the cliffs high above Ravenna Lake toward an obvious plateau at 6,400 feet. Please be aware of the exposure

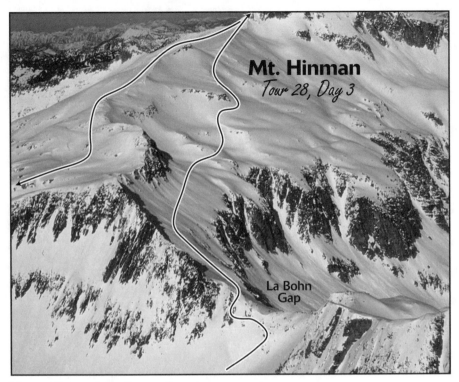

Mount Hinman from the southwest. PHOTO BY MARTIN VOLKEN

on this slope: A fall here might have dire consequences. It's equally important to have firm conditions when traversing this slope. Keep traversing east for about another kilometer (0.6 mile) until you see the easy slopes that let you gain the gentle west ridge of Mount Hinman at 7,280 feet. Follow the ridge and just left of the ridge in an easterly direction to the summit (7,495 feet).

To descend, you can retrace your ascent route. Be careful, however: Conditions at the cirque above Ravenna Lake change very quickly, since it gets a lot of sun exposure. Even a little sluff or a simple slip might carry you over the cliffs. You can also ski down the gentle west ridge high above Hinman Glacier. This is an easy, safe, and scenic descent and is probably the preferred option. You'll reach a little col between La Bohn Lakes and Chain Lakes. Turn south here to regain your ascent route and return to camp. The described descent route would of course make a very good ascent route as well, if conditions or your comfort level don't allow for the La Bohn Gap option.

## Day 4

This is a very scenic portion of the traverse. From camp start touring in a southerly direction up the hidden tributary valley that lies just west of the Summit Chief massif. At around 4,500 feet you'll break out into the open portion of this little valley. The impressive walls of Little, Middle, and Big Summit

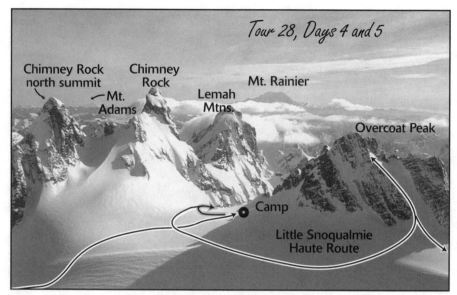

Chimney Rock group: Overcoat Peak and glacier from the northeast. PHOTO BY SCOTT
SCHELL

Chief will be on your left. Follow the valley up to the col (6,450 feet) just west of Summit Chief Mountain (2 to 3 hours to here). This col isn't named, but it's one of the key spots of the tour. You'll have spectacular views of the east face of Chimney Rock, the eastern edge of Overcoat Glacier, and some of the Lemah Towers.

From here you ski down in a southerly direction. Start out with a slight left-trending traverse until you're at about the 5,800-foot level. The terrain to your left will seem quite inviting, and skiing down that way certainly works. The safer option, however, is to orient yourself soft right to where the terrain seems to drop off steeply. You'll find a hidden entrance to a couloir that's objectively much safer than the open slope to your left.

Ski down to the 4,700-foot level, where the terrain flattens out (3 to 4 hours to here). Looking to the west-southwest, you'll see an old glacial trough that snakes up past Chimney Rock East Glacier and connects with a little tributary lobe coming off Overcoat Glacier. Tour up this until you gain a flat spot right below Chimney Rock's east face. At this point turn north-northwest until you reach the small but steep tributary lobe of Overcoat Glacier, and then the Overcoat Glacier plateau, by staying on the right side of tributary lobe.

If time and or conditions don't allow for this portion of the route, you can also traverse near the ridge that runs north–south from the Summit Chief saddle to the Overcoat Glacier plateau. (This ridge is the county and national forest boundary, as indicated on the map.) This ridge traverse is easy for the most part and will save you time, but note that it's exposed in a couple of short rocky sections near Overcoat Glacier.

From the Overcoat Glacier plateau turn southwest and tour the short distance to a distinct col between Overcoat Peak and the Chimney Rock massif at 6,800 feet (5.5 to 6.5 hours to here). Camp here.

## *Day 5*

This day starts with a somewhat committing ski descent into the Burntboot Creek valley. The upper part of the descent has a section that's at least 40 degrees, with much steeper slopes or cliffs (depending on conditions) below you. Ski down from your campsite for about 400 feet and start bearing right. This is the gentlest part of this fun but committing ski descent. Be careful: This would be an awkward spot to start a rescue.

Once you're down in the gentler part of the valley, continue to Iceberg Lake at 5,000 feet. You might hear the echo of your turns if the snow is firm enough (1 hour to here).

If you don't want to opt for the Overcoat col descent, you can circumnavigate Overcoat Peak counterclockwise, always staying above 6,400 feet. You'll eventually find an entrance into the Burntboot Creek valley just south of Overcoat Lake. This option is certainly more time consuming, but it's a safe way to go in questionable conditions.

Switch to tour mode at Iceberg Lake. Start skinning by skirting Iceberg Lake on its northeast side, then tour south below the west face of the Lemah Towers. You'll reach a little col by a knoll (indicated on the map as Point 6,022) (2 hours to here).

From this point traverse in a southerly direction until you reach the end of the Lemah Towers. Here at around 5,600 feet, you'll start touring uphill (bearing slightly west) in the direction of Chikamin Ridge. At around 6,400 feet change your bearing slightly eastward and gain the area below the two summit towers of Chikamin Peak (6,800 feet; about 5 hours to here). Deposit your skis here and climb up the short but steep gully to the summit notch. From here an easy and short scramble will put you on the summit of this great vista point (7,000 feet; about 6 hours to here).

If the summit notch is too corniced, you can try to circumnavigate the peak clockwise and approach the summit via its southeast slopes. There are plenty of options, but keep in mind that the upcoming descent off Chikamin Ridge is steep and south facing. Don't waste too much time trying to bag Chikamin Peak if it's late in the day.

Once you've returned to your ski depot, tour up to Chikamin Ridge and follow it along in a north-northwesterly direction to 6,840 feet. From here start skiing southwest to about 5,700 feet, and then start traversing to the west so you don't drop below the gentle ridge that extends from Huckleberry Mountain. Ski south from and pass slightly west of Point 5,524 on the map. Maintain your elevation and traverse until you come to the southeast ridge of Huckleberry Mountain. The east end of Joe Lake will lie right below you. Ski down and camp here (4,624 feet; 7 to 8 hours to here).

*Tour 28, Day 5*

**Hattrup and Volken below Chikamin Ridge from northeast.**

*Photo by Carl Skoog*

## Day 6

From Joe Lake tour up the beautiful wooded ridge to Alaska Peak's summit area. Traverse underneath Alaska Peak on its north side and gain the summit ridge of the mountain about 300 feet beyond the summit. Then you can tour the short distance on the ridge to its northernmost point (5,720 feet; about 1.5 hours to here).

From here ski down the other side, trying not to drop below 5,200 feet. Then start traversing directly west, passing two towers on the ridge to your right. Just beyond the second tower, you'll have to assess the snow stability and comfort level of your party. If conditions are good, you have a short but steep traverse above Alaska Lake and on to Ridge Lake at about 5,300 feet (2.5 hours to here). Be careful: A fall during this traverse might send you over the cliffs down to Alaska Lake. This slope is very avalanche prone. You must do this traverse in good conditions.

If you don't want to opt for the traverse, you'll have to boot-kick up to Bumblebee Pass, which lies up on the previously noted ridge just beyond the second tower. From here you drop into the beautiful Thompson basin, then start touring west and gain the ridge above Gravel Lake. If this ridge is very corniced, it may force you to tour to its northernmost point, just before the ridge starts to get rocky. From here ski down to Gravel Lake and then tour the short distance to Ridge Lake. Be careful: This descent is quite steep and the slopes might demand some flushing (about 3.5 to 4 hours to here).

From Ridge Lake keep traversing at about 5,400 feet on the south side of the ridge until the slope steepens below you. You're nearing a distinct spot on the Pacific Crest Trail called the Kendall Catwalk. In a time of lesser environmental awareness, the forest service blasted a short section of the trail right out of the rock face all the way to a pass north of Kendall Peak. If the trail is exposed, you've got it made (5,400 feet; 1 hour from Ridge Lake). If it's not (you can assess it from farther back on the slope), don't attempt a traverse unless the conditions are absolutely perfect. This slope is steep and slabby; it can be very dangerous. You'll be better off climbing up about 200 feet, where the terrain angles back a bit. From here you can traverse the short distance to a rocky ridge above the col where the Kendall Catwalk comes out. You'll have to down-climb the short distance on the ridge to get to the col (about 2 hours from Ridge Lake).

From the col ski down the little tributary drainage to the Commonwealth basin, staying generally on the south side of the creek. Once you're in the Commonwealth basin, ski out toward Snoqualmie Pass, staying on the east side of Commonwealth Creek. At the 3,500-foot level steer slightly east and away from the creek and you'll run into Alpental Road at 3,000 feet near I–90 and Snoqualmie Pass (5 to 8 hours from Joe Lake, depending on conditions).

This last day of the traverse travels through quite a bit of avalanche terrain and may force you to do several of the variations. Good conditions are crucial for this portion of the trip. If you don't like the conditions, you might be better off going down into the Gold Creek valley from Joe Lake and then skiing out to Hyak from there.

Tour 28, Day 6
**Peter Avolio and Andy Dappen on the infamous Kendall Catwalk.**
*Photo by Carl Skoog*

# A Bonus Tour

29

# The Forbidden Tour

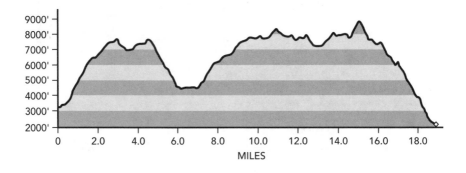

**Tour distance:** 36 km (19 miles)

**Tour time:** 3 to 4 days

**Vertical gain/loss:** 10,315 feet/11,234 feet

**Difficulty rating:** Grade IV-plus to V

**Best season:** April and May

**Starting elevation/high point:** 3,240 feet/8,868 feet

**Gear required:** Standard ski-mountaineering and overnight camping equipment

**Required fitness and skiing ability:** Excellent physical condition and expert skiing ability

**Maps needed:** Cascade Pass, Forbidden Peak, El Dorado Peak

The Forbidden Tour is one of the best tours I've come up with in the Northwest. It epitomizes everything that makes the North Cascades a great range to climb or to ski in. You'll be touring across seven glaciers of substantial size and drop deep into Washington wilderness. You'll find yourself touring, skiing, and camping in some of the most alpine environs found in the lower 48 states. You should be an experienced ski mountaineer and in very good physical condition.

You're essentially circumnavigating Forbidden Peak, and your commitment level increases substantially once you drop onto Boston Glacier. Observe the weather very carefully before you commit to Moraine Lake, since escape routes from there aren't easy. All things considered, the Forbidden Tour is a real ski-

MILES

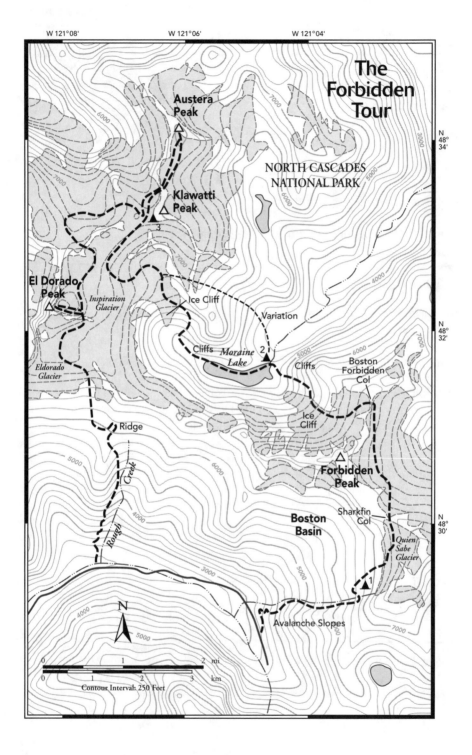

# The
# Forbidden
# Tour

Austera
Peak

NORTH CASCADES
NATIONAL PARK

Klawatti
Peak

3

El Dorado
Peak

*Inspiration
Glacier*

Ice Cliff

Variation

Cliffs

*Moraine
Lake*

2

Cliffs

Boston
Forbidden
Col

*Eldorado
Glacier*

Ice
Cliff

Ridge

Forbidden
Peak

*Rough Creek*

Boston
Basin

Sharkfin
Col

*Quien
Sabe
Glacier*

Avalanche Slopes

1

N

W 121°08'    W 121°06'    W 121°04'

N 48° 34'

N 48° 32'

N 48° 30'

0        1        2 mi
0    1    2    3 km
Contour Interval: 250 Feet

mountaineering adventure that requires skill and commitment.

**Permits:** Backcountry camping and climbing permits are required in North Cascades National Park and can be obtained at the ranger station in Marblemount (360–873–4500). You should also be able to obtain reliable information about Cascade River Road conditions at this number.

**Approach:** Take Interstate 5 to Burlington, getting off at the Cook Road exit (exit 232). Follow the signs to North Cascade Highway (Washington Highway 20) in Sedro Woolley, taking WA 20 for about 40 miles to Marblemount. Turn onto Cascade River Road and drive to the El Dorado Creek Trailhead at milepost 19 and 2,160 feet. Park here. If you have multiple vehicles, proceed past Gilbert's cabin to milepost 22 at 3,240 feet. This is the standard roadhead for the Boston basin approach. Park a second vehicle here and start your tour.

## Day 1

At the roadhead you're about 1 kilometer (0.6 mile) south of Midas Creek. Here the old Diamond Mine Road leads off to the north. Follow this road up. There will be several switchbacks in the road until it ends at 3,600 feet. From here tour up through steep terrain in an easterly direction for a few hundred feet until the terrain angles back at around 4,200 feet. Be careful in the ascent from 3,600 to 4,200 feet: It's quite steep, and the openness of the terrain in this otherwise timbered zone suggests regular avalanche activity. From 4,200 feet tour a bit more northeasterly until you're close to Midas Creek. Now you can follow the Midas Creek drainage upward until you're directly south of a very prominent knoll (Point 6,482 on the map). Tour up to the south of this knoll, and then gain its top by turning north at the 6,400-foot level (about 4 hours to here). It's crucial to get to this point early in the day, since the Midas Creek drainage is regularly flushed with avalanches.

From here proceed in a north-northeasterly direction to the northernmost tip of Quien Sabe Glacier. You'll be heading right for the Sharkfin col. There are a few hidden crevasses due to a small icefall about halfway between Point 6,482 and Sharkfin col. The glacier flattens out at the 7,500-foot level at the bottom of the col's couloir (about 5 hours to here). There's plenty of room for safe and scenic camping. This spot will put you in a great position for the Sharkfin col crossing the next day, or a western variation of the tour if the weather doesn't look reliable.

## Day 2

From camp climb up the obvious couloir toward the Sharkfin col. From the bottom of the couloir, there's another distinct and steep gully that leads off slightly more to the right. If you go up this way, you'll get around the rock scramble, but the descent on the other side will be difficult and time consuming.

So climb up the obvious couloir, negotiating the bergschrund at the bottom. Keep climbing until you run out of snow. At this point the left side of the

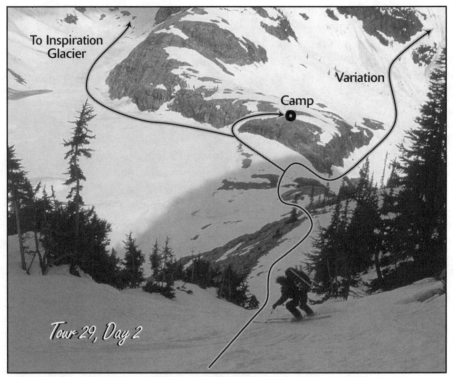

To Inspiration Glacier

Variation

Camp

Tour 29, Day 2

Jeff Hansell approaching the camp at Moraine Lake. PHOTO BY SCOTT SCHELL

gully seems inviting, since it's less steep—but don't go there. The rock quality is highly questionable. Instead, stay on the right border of the gully and climb up the obvious rocky ledges. Toward the top of the gully, the terrain angles back but the rock quality deteriorates again. Careful movement and appropriate people management are crucial in this couloir.

You'll climb up to an obvious belay block at the very top of the gully and to climber's right of a little tower. This block is equipped with anchor slings of various ages and quality (7,760 feet; 1 hour to here).

The anchor block works very well for belays from the Quien Sabe side and the rappel down to the Boston Glacier side. This point in the tour is an important one, since a retreat is potentially difficult once you're on Boston Glacier. If you don't like the weather or general conditions, you should probably make the call here.

**Variation:** You can retreat down the gully to Quien Sabe Glacier and start skiing and traversing in a west-northwesterly direction toward a little col on the western border of the Boston basin. This col is located on the rib that's essentially a continuation of Mount Torment's south ridge (6,620 feet; about 1 hour from camp). Be sure to check out the steep slope leading up to the pass when you're touring up Quien Sabe Glacier on day 1. The orientation of the rib makes it prone to massive cornices.

From the col continue in a northwesterly direction underneath the south face of Mount Torment to gain the gentle ridge that trends away from Mount Torment toward the El Dorado plateau. Once you're on the ridge, you'll have plenty of alternatives for the tour.

From the top of Sharkfin col, make the short rappel down to Boston Glacier and ski in a northerly direction to the toe of the prominent rib at 7,100 feet. From here tour up and across Boston Glacier, still heading in a northerly direction, to the northernmost extension of Forbidden Peak's north ridge (7,600 feet; about 4 hours to here). You'll see a steep but short slope that leads up to the easternmost edge of Forbidden Glacier. It's important to get here early in the day. This short slope is very steep at the top and has full eastern exposure. Climb up the slope and exit it on its left side by a crumbly-looking rock horn. this puts you onto Forbidden Glacier at 7,700 feet (5 hours to here).

From this col ski down Forbidden Glacier on its northern side. (There's no other way to say it: This section rules.) At around 5,600 you'll have to make the call whether to ski down to the snout of the glacier or to move farther north into some little trees. The glacier option is less steep, but there are big cliffs toward the bottom, and you'll be subjecting yourself to avalanche and icefall danger from the Mount Torment and Forbidden Peak cliffs high above. Skiing through the trees is probably safer if the snow conditions on the actual slope leading down to Moraine Lake are good. Keep in mind that you'll be skiing down 40-degree terrain that's slabby in summer. Terrain and condition assessment is of the essence. This fantastic ski descent will bring you down to the eastern edge of Moraine Lake. Right next to the lake outflow are some beautiful campsites (4,530 feet; about 6 hours to here).

## Day 3

You have to feel good about avalanche danger, weather, and the conditions on the lake if you want to reach the Inspiration plateau via the Moraine Lake crossing. If you're not confident about things, you have a couple of options:

**Option 1:** You battle it out in the Thunder Creek valley and make it out to Diablo Lake that way. Be aware that a descent down the West Fork of Thunder Creek bears its own dangers, and the following slog through the swampy Thunder Creek lowlands could turn into a sporty event. This is a last-resort option, to say the least.

**Option 2:** This is probably the more realistic option. From your campsite ski down the short section to a big flat area at 4,200 feet. Now traverse north-northwest for about 1 kilometer (0.6 mile), then turn northwest up the slope toward the eastern border of the massive Inspiration cirque. The slope you're about to tour up is huge and can produce massive slides. Be careful: If you don't trust the conditions on the slope, you might be better off sitting tight at

**Don Denton approaching the lower
Inspiration Glacier Plateau.**

*Photo by Martin Volken*

Moraine Lake until things improve. (But heck, that's why it's called the Forbidden Tour.) You'll reach the ridge that lets you drop onto the Inspiration side
at around 7,200 feet. From there you can proceed directly to the Klawatti col
by staying high by the ridge (about 5 hours from camp).

From your camp at Moraine Lake, ski across the lake toward the distinct
lobe of Inspiration Glacier that reaches down to nearly 5,200 feet. When you're
about 1 kilometer (0.6 mile) northwest of the lake, you'll see that the terrain
angles back a bit to the north. Tour and climb up this slope to about 5,400 feet
(1.5 to 2 hours to here). The terrain becomes tourable again from this point on.
Tour west and northwest from here. Within a short time you'll find yourself
above some sizable cliffs—which may remind you that the inventor of the ski
crampon is a hero. Keep touring in this northwesterly direction and gain the
easy entrance to Inspiration Glacier at 6,000 feet. This entrance is an important
one, but it's easy to find. If you're too low, the passage will be blocked by ice
cliffs; if you're too high, you'll run into untourably steep and rocky terrain (6,050
feet; 2.5 to 3 hours to here).

From here you have two options:

**Option 1:** If conditions are favorable and the snow is still firm enough, you can keep touring up this gentle portion of Inspiration Glacier in a northwesterly direction. This will lead you to the bottom of a very distinct couloir at 6,700 feet. Ascend this couloir and continue straight north to the Klawatti col at 7,800 feet (5 hours to here).

**Option 2:** In this option you essentially make a clockwise turn around the cliff and icefall located west of the couloir described in Option 1. Tour away from the passage, also in a northwesterly direction, until you reach the 6,600-foot level. Here you turn west and ascend upper Inspiration Glacier to about 7,600 feet. Then turn northeast and tour the remaining 2 kilometers (1.2 miles) to the Klawatti col. Be aware that your direction of travel is parallel to some sizable crevasses (about 6 hours to here). Make camp here at the Klawatti col.

If time and energy allow it you can make the quick excursion to Austera Peak. This will reward you with views into the spectacular icefalls of McAllister Glacier. From camp tour along the west side of Klawatti Peak and cross from McAllister Glacier to Klawatti Glacier right by the toe of Klawatti Peak's north ridge (7,900 feet). Now tour in a northerly direction on Klawatti Glacier to the first summit tower of Austera Peak. Just before you get to the top of what you might assume is the summit, deposit your skis (at around 8,300 feet), drop onto the west side of the tower, and follow below an easy but potentially corniced ridge for about 100 feet to the notch of the true summit tower. A short but exposed chimney through rock and snow will get you to the top of Austera Peak (8,334 feet; 2 hours from the Klawatti col). If time seems a little short, you might consider simply going to the satellite summit. The views are just as good, and you won't have to commit to a climb late in the day.

To descend, down-climb or rappel to the notch and then retrace the short traverse to your ski depot. From here return to camp via your ascent track (about 3 hours from the Klawatti col).

Austera Peak is obviously just one of the options you could use for "afternoon entertainment." Here are some other suggestions: a circumnavigation of Klawatti Peak, an ascent of the smokestack on Klawatti's north ridge, or a simple ski down Klawatti Glacier toward Klawatti Lake. Ascending the tempting South Couloir of Klawatti Peak isn't a good option this late in the day, but it would be a fantastic start tomorrow.

# Day 4

If you decide to climb up the South Couloir of Klawatti Peak, you must get an early start. From camp tour to the south side of the mountain and ascend the obvious broad couloir to the summit flanks, then on to the summit. If conditions are right, this ascent route is certainly skiable.

Upon returning to your campsite, break down camp and start touring south toward the east ridge of El Dorado Peak, maintaining an elevation of about 7,800 feet. Once you reach the east ridge (about 1 hour from camp), deposit unnecessary gear, then turn west and tour up the broad east ridge. Good terrain management and a few kick turns will bring you to the base of the short

El Dorado Glacier

To
Roush Creek

*Tour 29, Day 4*

El Dorado Peak from the northeast. PHOTO BY MARTIN VOLKEN

summit ridge (8,750 feet; about 2.5 hours to here). Deposit your skis here and climb the short but exposed snow ridge to the summit of El Dorado Peak (8,868 feet; about 3 hours to here).

It's all downhill from here—nearly 6,700 feet of it. From the summit climb back down to your skis, and then ski the very enjoyable east ridge back to your gear cache at 7,800 feet. From here ski across the east ridge and the southernmost portion of the Inspiration plateau in a southerly direction to El Dorado Glacier (7,400 feet; about 4.5 to 5 hours to here). Now continue skiing in a southeasterly direction along the rib that divides the Roush Creek drainage from the El Dorado Creek drainage (you're skiing on its west side). At 6,150 feet you'll find an easy crossing to the other side of the rib. This spot is important. You're now in the El Dorado Creek drainage. Ski down this drainage, staying generally west of the creek. The terrain gets steeper at around 4,800 feet. You're entering a big talus zone that might not hold all that much snow anymore. At 4,000 feet the terrain gets steeper still. Continue to stay west of the creek, and you should find the climber's trail fairly easily (3,800 feet; about 6 hours to here).

Follow this climber's trail down into the valley. The trail will lead you to a solid log crossing across the Cascade River about 300 feet west of the El Dorado Trail car park (2,160 feet; about 7.5 to 8 hours to here). You're there—you did it.

# Appendix

Following is some information for getting professional guidance and purchasing the appropriate gear for ski touring in this region.

## Ski and Mountain Shops

The following list isn't complete. It is a selection of shops that will provide you with high quality ski-touring gear and professional advice.

**Marmot Mountain Works**
827 Bellevue Way NE
Bellevue, WA 98004
(425) 453–1515

**Pro Ski Service/North Bend**
108 West North Bend Way
North Bend, WA 98045
(425) 888–6397

**Pro Ski Service/Seattle**
8954 Aurora Avenue North
Seattle, WA 98103
(206) 525–4425

**Feathered Friends**
119 Yale Avenue North
Seattle, WA 98109
(206) 292–2210

## Ski Guides and Ski-Mountaineering Guides

For a complete list of educated and qualified guides, please consult the guides roster found on the Web page of the American Mountain Guides Association: www.amga.com.

Pro Guiding Service is currently the only guiding outfit that leads ski mountaineering trips into the Chimney Rock area and to the Forbidden Tour. It is located at 108 West North Bend Way, North Bend, WA 98045; (425) 888–6397; www.proguiding.com.

## About the Author

Martin Volken was born and raised in Switzerland. He grew up in the village of Stalden outside Zermatt. This is where he received his formal training as a Swiss Mountain Guide. He moved to the Seattle area in the late 1980s. He is the owner of Pro Ski Service and Pro Guiding Service, which operates ski, rock, and alpine climbing trips in North America and the Alps. He works as an instructor/examiner for the ski mountaineering program of the American Mountain Guides Association.